Uppark Restored

Uppark Restored

CHRISTOPHER ROWELL

AND

JOHN MARTIN ROBINSON

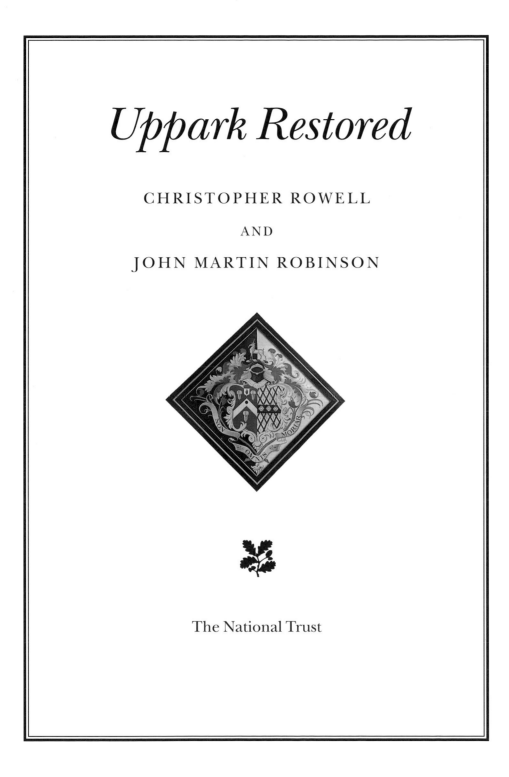

The National Trust

First published in Great Britain in 1996
by National Trust Enterprises Limited,
36 Queen Anne's Gate, London SW1H 9AS

British Library Cataloguing in Publication Data
A catalogue record for this book is available from the British Library.

ISBN 0 7078 0252 0 hardback
ISBN 0 7078 0213 X paperback

Frontispiece:
The restored south front at Uppark. Because the 1989 fire vented through the roof rather than the windows, the brickwork emerged remarkably unscathed. Even lichens remain, giving the house an uncanny look of being untouched by the fire.

Title page:
The funeral hatchment of Mary Ann Bullock, wife of Sir Harry Fetherstonhaugh: Fetherstonhaugh impaled by her arms created after their marriage in 1825. This hatchment would have hung on the front of Uppark at her death in 1874, and thereafter in South Harting church. The motto, very appropriate to Uppark, is *Non Omnis Moriar* (I shall not wholly die).

Edited by Sarah Riddell

Designed by Peter Guy

Production Management by Bob Towell

Phototypeset in New Baskerville
by Southern Positives and Negatives (SPAN), Lingfield, Surrey

Printed and bound in Italy by Grafedit S.p.A., Bergamo

Contents

Authors' acknowledgements

In the rescue and repair of Uppark, the National Trust has incurred many debts: to those who fought the fire or rescued contents; to the workers who retrieved fragments from the ruins; to the conservators for emergency and subsequent work; to the architects, contractors, builders and craftsmen who designed or carried out the repairs. The Trust is also grateful to English Heritage for providing the services of its archaeological team, and to H.M. The Queen and the Royal Collection Trust for providing help with emergency picture conservation after the fire. Sun Alliance, which, as the Sun Fire Office, first insured Uppark in 1753, has worked closely with the Trust and sponsored the Sun Alliance Exhibition & Visitor Centre as well as various Uppark publications. The exhibition chronicles the restoration of Uppark from the fire on 30 August 1989 through to its reopening on 1 June 1995.

For help with this book, we are primarily indebted to the Meade-Fetherstonhaugh family for permission to consult and publish documents in their possession, and to Timothy McCann, who administers the family archive in the West Sussex Record Office at Chichester. Tracey Avery and Nino Strachey undertook most of the initial archival research. We are grateful to those who have read the whole, or sections, of the text in draft, and who have made valuable comments, and to those who have helped in other ways: Fred Aldsworth, Lady Jean Babington-Smith, Anna Bennett, Ian Constantinides, Harriet de Bianchi Cossart, Martin Drury, Guy Evans, John Eyre, Emma Goad, Catherine Hassall, Sukie Hemming, Richard Henderson, Simon Jervis, Allyson McDermott, Iain McLaren, Mrs Richard Meade-Fetherstonhaugh, Martin Mortimer, Christine Palmer, Peter Pearce, Julian Prideaux, Trevor Proudfoot, Nigel Seeley, David Sekers, Jonathan Tetley, Sophie Warre, Robert Weston, Mr and Mrs Samuel Whitbread, Kevin Whitehead, Margaret Willes, Jeremy Wood, Annabel Wylie. Conall MacFarlane, Timothy Hunter and their colleagues at Christies have given valuable advice on aspects of the collection.

Jillie Miller and Delores Karney typed our manuscripts with considerable accuracy. For general assistance and in the procurement of photographs, we are indebted to Sophie Blair, Charles O'Brien, Ian Constantinides, Dan Cruikshank, Richard Ireland, Delores Karney, Alan Lamb, Christine Marshall, Trevor Proudfoot, Nigel Seeley, Matthew Slocombe, John Thorneycroft, Andrew Townend, Philip Venning and Morwenna Wallis.

Finally, for her expertise in blending and distilling our contributions, we owe a special debt of gratitude to our editor, Sarah Riddell.

Picture acknowledgements

The authors and publishers are grateful to the following for providing illustrations and giving permission for their reproduction.

Sheila Atkinson: 16 above left and right, below; Colin Birt: 124 above left and right, below left and right; Michael Chevis: 58, 91, 114 left; Cliveden Conservation Workshop: 87 left, centre and right, 157 right, 167 left; C. Cormack: 84 left; Country Life Picture Library: 23 below left, 40 above, 49 left, 64, 74 above, 109 above left; Rupert Harris: 149 left; A. F. Kersting: 141 left, 173 left, 176 right; John Mills: 97; Sheila Orme: 104 below; Portsmouth Publishing & Printing Ltd: 17, 27, 85 right; Paul Reeves: 143 above; RIBA: 51, 55 below, 75; Christopher Rowell: 149 centre; Royal Commission for Historical Monuments: 95 left, 101 above right; The Conservation Practice: 42, 43, 50, 52, 70, 151; West Sussex Record Office: 45, 57 below; Hamilton Weston Wallpaper: 127.

National Trust Photographic Library (Queen Anne's Gate): 11, 31, 85 left, 118, 137, 175 right; Matthew Antrobus: frontispiece; Peter Aprahamian: 95 right; David Bradfield: 25 right, 28, 68 above, 145 above right; Andrew Butler: 36 right; Prudence Cuming: 55 above, 57 above; Patsy Fagan: 21, 23 above left, 25 left, 101 above left; Geoffrey Frosh: 47 left, 103, 111 right; John Hammond: 65, 133 right, 136; Angelo Hornak: 129, 144, 158; Nadia Mackenzie: title page, 94 below, 115, 133 left, 139, 162, 164, 177; Ian West: 8, 14, 23 right; Jeremy Whitaker: 110, 111 left, 112; Andreas von Einsiedel: 84 below right.

National Trust Regional Libraries and Archives: 36 left, 37 left and right, 53, 63 right, 123, 133 centre, 141 right, 149 right, 172, 175 left, 176 left; Mark Fiennes: 174; David Levenson: 179; Robin Ross: 167 right; Tim Stephens: 19, 26, 29, 40 below, 41, 47 right, 49 right, 60, 61, 63 left, 66, 68 below, 74 below, 79, 88 above and below left, 93 left, 104 above, 106, 109 above right and below, 114 right, 116–7, 119 above, 125, 130, 134, 145 above left and below, 147 above and below, 153 left and right, 154, 155 above and below, 157 left, 159, 161 above and below, 169, 180; Rupert Truman: 72, 77, 81, 83 left and right, 84 above right, 88 right, 90, 93 right, 94 above, 99, 101 below left and right, 119 below, 143 below left and right; Robin Ross: 173 right.

Some of the illustrations were taken before the fire at Uppark or during the rescue and conservation of the house and its collection: they are of historical value, but are, naturally, not always of the highest technical quality.

Foreword

'NEXT THERE CAME A LOW RUMBLE, sparks flying like fireworks ...,
and the whole of Uptake was roaring and crackling.' These words describe
the climax of a story published in 1944, strangely prefiguring the fire that
ravaged Uppark forty-five years later. *The Last of Uptake* by Simon Harcourt-
Smith, with illustrations by Rex Whistler, is a picaresque novel about a
country house called Uptake, the home of two old ladies, the last of their
line, who set it on fire to prevent it from passing into other hands. Rex
Whistler's tailpiece shows the sisters driving away in their carriages with the
great house ablaze in the distance.

In the dying years of the nineteenth century Uppark was also the home
of two old ladies, the owner Miss Fetherstonhaugh and her companion.
Miss Fetherstonhaugh chose a different solution to the future of Uppark,
however. She bequeathed it to the son of a neighbour who, as Admiral the
Hon. Sir Herbert Meade-Fetherstonhaugh, came into his inheritance in
1931. It was Uppark's good fortune that he and his wife were to devote the
next thirty-five years to the careful preservation of a house on which time
had laid an unusually light hand.

Uppark is seven miles from the nearest fire station and for two centuries
depended on the erratic performance of a ram to raise its water supply from
a pond at the bottom of Harting Hill. The fear of fire was therefore ever-
present and those who were invited to Lady Meade-Fetherstonhaugh's
Christmas parties for local children recall that, as she handed out presents
beneath a great candle-lit tree in the hall, it was the duty of the Admiral and
his son to stand by with wet sponges on the end of sticks, ready to douse the
candles as they burned low. Many years later, these precautions were to
prove well founded.

In the late afternoon of 30 August 1989 I was in my office at the London
headquarters of the National Trust in Queen Anne's Gate when the news
came of a fire at Uppark. No details were known and the Uppark telephone
was giving the engaged signal. Having learned the lesson of the Hampton
Court fire three years before, we had set up a telephone 'tree', a procedure
by which each of the Trust's conservation advisers would telephone another
before going as quickly as possible to the scene of an emergency.

The 'tree' was duly activated and I set off for Uppark with Sukie Hemming,

Uppark burning on the
night of 30 August 1989.

[9]

a member of staff who happened to have her car at the office. As the grand-daughter of Admiral and Lady Meade-Fetherstonhaugh, Sukie had spent much of her childhood at Uppark, and because I had care of it in the 1970s as the Trust's local representative, it was more familiar to me than most other National Trust houses. We drove most of the way in a state of silent apprehension. At the village of Rogate we began to strain our eyes for smoke above the line of the South Downs ahead. A fire-engine passed, travelling at speed in the opposite direction. We took this as a sign that if there had been a fire it was out, but later learned it had been one of many reconnoitring Sussex in search of water.

On Harting Hill there were firemen and hoses on the road, draining the old mill pond at the bottom. Talking our way through the police at the gate, we went up the long drive with sinking hearts and turned in at Repton's Golden Gates. All I remember of the sight which confronted us then is the jagged roofless silhouette of the house, with its chimneys standing un-naturally tall against the sky and smoke streaming away before a south-west wind: a scene of devastation beyond the worst we had feared. Flames were crackling behind the windows of the first floor, firemen were playing hoses from high ladders and on the ground the first firefighter to whom I spoke told us that there would be nothing left by the time the fire was under control. That, at least, was to prove too pessimistic a prophecy.

The upper floors and everything in them had been destroyed, but most of the contents of the show-rooms on the ground floor and basement had been rescued by the firemen, helped by members of staff, volunteers and the Meade-Fetherstonhaugh family, and were safely stored in out-build-ings. I walked round the house looking in to see what remained. In the Stone Hall, a few feet away from the open door, stood the pair of tables with scagliola tops, commissioned in Florence in the 1750s by Sir Matthew Fetherstonhaugh during his Grand Tour. They were among the finest things of their kind, but had been abandoned because it was thought that they were attached to their carved wood rococo frames screwed to the wall. I urged a quick dash to seize the tops and bring them out; sparks and frag-ments of plaster were falling and I remember the wise response of the Chief Fire Officer: 'There's no way my men are going in there now.' Days later, the tables were recovered in pieces from beneath a metre of ash, rubble and charred beams.

Today, those tables stand once again where they were that evening, bearing the scars of their ordeal, but painstakingly pieced together, their missing parts replaced. They are a symbol of the determination we all felt to defy the forces of destruction, to make good the appalling damage and to ensure that in years to come the fire of 1989 would come to be seen as no more than another incident in the long history of the house. They are a tribute, too, to the skill and resourcefulness of the hundreds of people who played a part in making a reality of that instinctive response to catastrophe.

Lady Meade-Fetherston-haugh with her daughter, now Lady Jean Babington-Smith. This photograph of *c*.1935, shows the two ladies displaying damask curtains before and after conservation. After washing the curtains in extract of *saponaria*, a process that sometimes included dragging them over the dewy grass, the frayed silk was stitched down or 'couched'.

One happy consequence of the five-year campaign of repair described in this book is the revelation that, contrary to the opinion too often heard, craftsmanship is far from dead. Visitors to Uppark today can see the work of craftsmen and women of the 1990s beside that of their eighteenth-century predecessors and they are indistinguishable. The truth is that the skills exist or are latent; all that is needed is the will, and the money to pay for them.

There is one question still to be answered. Has the soul of Uppark survived? Has its atmosphere been affected by the trauma of August 1989? Only visitors who knew it before can judge, but those who were working on the project could not help being both reassured and moved by a letter received soon after the roof had gone back in 1992. The writer was Lady Jean Babington-Smith, whose childhood home Uppark had been. After her first visit since the fire she wrote: 'I had been in such trepidation before my visit, expecting a parody ... I went for a walk down the West Drive and looked back. The house seemed the same as ever: still my old friend.'

Martin Drury
Director-General
The National Trust

*c.*1690   Uppark rebuilt in the Anglo-Dutch tradition, possibly to the design of William Talman, by Ford Grey, 3rd Lord Grey of Warke (created Earl of Tankerville in 1695). The exterior and ground-plan of the house essentially unchanged to this day.

1701   On Lord Tankerville's death, Uppark inherited by his only child Mary, married to Charles Bennet (created 1st Earl of Tankerville, of the second creation, in 1714), owner of estates in Northumberland and Middlesex.

1722   Uppark passed to Charles, 2nd Earl of Tankerville, a soldier and courtier whose wife became Lady of the Bedchamber to Queen Caroline, consort of King George II. Two views of the house and estate by Pieter Tillemans (before 1734) installed in the panelling of the Staircase Hall.

1747   Uppark sold for £19,000 to Sir Matthew Fetherstonhaugh, a cultivated Northumbrian baronet who had recently inherited £400,000. First phase of extensive remodelling and refurnishing of Uppark. His marriage in 1746 to Sarah Lethieullier, from a prominent Huguenot banking family, immortalised in the series of portraits by Arthur Devis (1748 and 1749) and by Pompeo Batoni (1751 and 1752).

1749–51 Sir Matthew and Lady Fetherstonhaugh's Grand Tour of the Continent. Most of the pictures and the scagliola-topped tables (Stone Hall) acquired or commissioned.

1754–8 Fetherstonhaugh House (now the Scottish Office), in Whitehall, built for Sir Matthew by the architect James Paine, whose influence is detected in the rococo-style redecoration at Uppark in the late 1740s and 1750s.

*c.*1770   The final – and most splendid – phase of Sir Matthew's redecoration of Uppark, including the Saloon and Little Parlour, again probably to the design of Paine.

1774   Sir Harry Fetherstonhaugh succeeded to the title and property on his father's death. A taste for the decorative arts, acquired on a Grand Tour, displayed in his fine collection of French furniture, clocks and porcelain. In 1780–1 Uppark was host to Sir Harry's mistress, Emma, the future Lady Hamilton, in 1784–5 and subsequently to the Prince of Wales (later George IV), whom Sir Harry advised on the acquisition of works of art.

1810   Humphry Repton's Red Book set out proposals for alterations to Uppark.

1811–15   Repton's alterations for Sir Harry included moving Uppark's main entrance from the east to the north, with a new Portland stone portico; a stone-coloured vaulted passage to the Staircase Hall; the Dining Room remodelled in seventeenth-century style; and a Servery lit by a stained-glass window. Repton also repainted the Saloon white and gold.

1825   Sir Harry's marriage to his dairy-maid, Mary Ann Bullock, fifty years his junior; her sister Frances joined the ménage soon afterwards. Some redecoration carried out between 1825 and 1846.

1846   On Sir Harry's death, his widow and her sister devoted themselves to Uppark. In the 1850s and 1860s crimson flock wallpapers purchased and some repainting commissioned. On the death of her sister in 1874, Frances Bullock inherited Uppark and adopted the name Fetherstonhaugh.

1895   Uppark bequeathed to Colonel the Hon. Keith Turnour (who took the name Fetherstonhaugh).

1930   Under the terms of Miss Fetherstonhaugh's will, Uppark passed to Admiral the Hon. Sir Herbert Meade (who became Meade-Fetherstonhaugh). Lady Meade-Fetherstonhaugh's careful preservation of Uppark's textiles, decoration and furnishings ensured their remarkable survival.

1954   Uppark passed to the National Trust by the gift of Admiral Meade-Fetherstonhaugh and his son Richard, with the family continuing to live in the house as tenants. The family's policy of preserving Uppark with as little change as possible continued by the Trust.

1989   August; fire severely damaged Uppark's state rooms; the Meade-Fetherstonhaughs' upstairs apartments and their contents totally destroyed.

1995   Uppark reopened to visitors in the National Trust's centenary year.

_1_ : _The Fire and Salvage_

WEDNESDAY 30 AUGUST 1989 was warm and windy. Although the sun was shining in a cloudless sky, there was a strong south-westerly breeze: typical August weather on this exposed crest of the South Downs in West Sussex. Uppark's brick and stone walls had been shrouded in scaffolding for over a year, but this was due to be dismantled the following day on completion of structural and roof repairs. A small team of leadworkers were sunning themselves and drinking tea on the lawn when they noticed a puff of smoke on the roof. The fire-alarms in the house sounded at 3.36pm. There had been 270 visitors that afternoon; those remaining in the house were swiftly evacuated and the gates were opened on the north drive to allow the fire-engines to pass. The alarm was linked via a monitoring agency to the local fire stations at Petersfield, at Midhurst and to the county headquarters at Chichester. It seemed at first to be a practice – there was no evidence of a fire within the building. But the smoke was soon more pronounced. The leadworkers, subcontracted to Haden Young Ltd, had been welding sheets of lead on the roof adjoining the pediment; contrary to instructions, they had left the scaffolding prematurely, thereby failing to detect the ignition of the timbers beneath the lead. By the time they had returned, their fire extinguisher was powerless to arrest the progress of the fire, which was already spreading through the roof cavity.

A remarkable series of photographs taken by a visitor to the house charts the progress of the fire. Eight minutes after the fire-alarm had sounded, smoke was billowing from the east side of the pediment; soon afterwards the first flames were visible and then spread; by 4 o'clock a fireman's hose created clouds of steam. The first engine had arrived from Petersfield a few minutes earlier, and had immediately radioed for two more. The Midhurst engine followed a minute later and summoned a further two. Within half an hour there were four fire-engines at Uppark and a further sixteen on their way. At the height of the fire, there were 27 fire-engines and 156 firemen, from West Sussex, Hampshire and Surrey.

Kenneth Lloyd, then Deputy Chief Fire Officer for West Sussex, took charge at 4.25pm. He immediately realised that the fire would burn inexorably from the roof to the basement and bought time for the salvage of the contents. The evacuation of the pictures, furniture, textiles and fittings was already under way. The contents of the Little Parlour were cleared by a team

Uppark burning on the night of 30 August 1989.

Three images from the
series of photographs by
Sheila Atkinson recording
the swift progress of the
fire: (*above left*) leadworkers returning to
the scaffolding at about
3.45pm, 30 August 1989;
(*above right*) the fire taking
hold in the roof space;
(*below*) 4.15pm, visitors
evacuated from the house
watching helplessly.
The house had been in
scaffolding for almost a
year, with the roof repairs
practically complete.

of house staff and volunteer room stewards. The Saloon was next: the great
glass doors to the south steps were thrown open, and English and French
furniture, books and porcelain were brought out and piled up on the grass.

Earlier on, a team of firemen had been led upstairs to the seat of the fire
but were beaten back by the flames in the attic. As they rushed down the

A swift response by staff, volunteer room stewards and the Meade-Fetherstonhaugh family, co-ordinated by the fire brigade, made possible the rescue of a remarkably large proportion of the contents of the house. Tragically, the private collection of the first floor was lost, as were several heavy and fixed pieces of furniture on the ground floor.

corridor, the ceiling collapsed in a shower of sparks and burning timbers. On their retreat, they snatched up an eighteenth-century portrait of a dog. This proved to be the sole survivor of the private collection, because by the time that it was clear that the fire would engulf the Meade-Fetherstonhaugh family's first-floor rooms it was too dangerous to evacuate their contents. Instead, tragically as it turned out, pictures were moved from one end of the first floor to the other rather than being taken downstairs. By 4.30pm the fire was already breaking through from the attic, and half an hour later the family apartment was a mass of flames which were seen licking through the closed windows. The destruction of these magical panelled or wallpapered rooms, largely untouched since the eighteenth century, with their outstanding seventeenth-, eighteenth- and early nineteenth-century paintings, furniture and textiles, was the greatest disaster of the fire.

It was apparent, from the beginning of the desperate fire-fighting campaign, that Uppark's hill-top situation would create huge problems in the procurement of water. Uppark had depended upon wells and dew ponds until before 1746, when a water supply had been 'sometime since erected' by means of lead pipes and an engine within the existing pump-house at the foot of the steep hill on the outskirts of South Harting, over a mile away; in 1731 a payment was made for 'looking after the Water Engine'. By 4.30pm on that August afternoon the water supply was already giving out. While the Dairy tank and the Meade-Fetherstonhaugh family's swimming pool were drained, five fire-engines and a hose-layer laid pipes down the hill to South Harting. But the South Harting main soon collapsed under the pressure and the firemen on the scaffold pouring water through the disintegrating roof saw their jets diminish into a trickle.

From about 5 o'clock and throughout the night, six fire-engines and two 5,000 gallon water-carriers shuttled between a 5in (13cm) main a few miles away and Uppark, where they off-loaded into holding tanks near the north drive gates. Also, firemen foraging for water found a private fishing lake in a wood near the village. The fire-engines could not reach it, so the water was transferred via a pipe through the wood to the line of fire-engines pumping water up South Harting hill. The following morning the lake was almost dry, and the shallow water was teeming with fish.

This resolute search for water did not hamper the rescue of the contents, but there were three worrying moments when the supply of water failed, and inevitably valuable time was lost. Soon after 5 o'clock, fire-crews wearing breathing apparatus went through the north entrance and under a protective shower of water scooped up the set of portraits by Arthur Devis and a painting of Sir Matthew Fetherstonhaugh's racehorses by John Boultbee from the east wall of the burning Staircase Hall. Further up the stairs, it was impossible to save a large painting of the battle of Trafalgar, whose surface was flayed from the stretcher in the searing heat. At ground-floor level, despite the danger of falling timbers and showers of burning lead, the firemen, wielding crowbars, prised Pieter Tillemans's huge pair of Uppark landscapes from the panelling in which they had been set in the 1720s. Minutes later, the staircase collapsed in a welter of flame. Other salvage teams, an officer and four or five men, went in continuously with designated paintings or other objects in view. In the Saloon, two large paintings from Luca Giordano's Prodigal Son series were hauled down from their positions high on the north wall. Luckily, the gilt fillets which held them in place were easily detached, allowing the canvases to be swiftly removed

Prophet and Surprise, two of Sir Matthew's race-horses, painted by John Boultbee. This picture was rescued *in extremis* from the Staircase Hall, where the fire burned fiercely. The varnish is blanched by water from the firemen's hoses, but the damage was comparatively easily rectified in the course of studio treatment.

from the plasterwork. Until about 6 o'clock, the firemen made rapid sorties into the stricken building to rescue what they could.

Earlier, a news cameraman in a helicopter had filmed the plume of smoke swirling to the north-east. The lens focused on the ant-like figures running in and out of the house, fighting the flames or rescuing contents. These were the pictures that appeared on that evening's television news. The footage clearly showed that the roof had collapsed and that the attic was ruined, with its wooden floor in flames. The first floor was also ablaze. The contents on the grass were gradually taken under cover – into the Stables on the west side or into the former Orangery, Kitchen and Laundry Block (the present tea-room) to the east. By 6 o'clock, when most of the obviously portable objects had been removed, there was a lull. The ground-floor state-rooms were still intact, the fire was raging above and it was obvious that it would soon break through and destroy Uppark's grandest interiors.

At National Trust regional and national headquarters, the alarm had been raised by press inquiries. Soon, switchboards were jammed with calls from reporters, thereby hampering the communication of the disaster and the summons of help from experts within and without the Trust. A disaster plan, revised since the 1986 fire at Hampton Court, was put into operation. Telephone calls were made to an array of conservators; supplies of equipment (bubble wrap, tissue paper, blotting paper) were hurriedly amassed; a Land-Rover filled with salvage equipment was despatched from Kingston Lacy in Dorset.

When David Sekers, Director of the National Trust's Southern Region and Christopher Rowell, regional Historic Buildings Representative, arrived at Uppark at about 6.30pm, they were hoping that the uncon-firmed news of the fire would turn out to be a false alarm. On the drive their worst fears were confirmed as they first smelled and then saw the smoke. Having reported immediately to Kenneth Lloyd, they made a rapid circuit of the building to assess the success of the salvage operation. This had been an heroic effort, but it was clear that the state-rooms were on the point of destruction, and that the less obviously portable objects – fixed furniture, pier-glasses and curtains, as well as fixtures and fittings, wallpapers and decorative woodwork – would be totally destroyed unless a second phase of salvage was attempted. The interior had long been out of bounds to anyone other than firemen, and despite the increasing danger, the Chief Salvage Officer detailed a group of firemen to respond to National Trust requests for rescue attempts.

Still hanging at the windows were the red and yellow silk damask festoon curtains, believed to date from the eighteenth century. It was possible for individual firemen to reach up and tear down the curtains from the wooden pelmet boards to which they were close-nailed. The fact that most of these fragile curtains were robust enough to come down in one piece was due to their conservation in the 1930s by Lady (Margaret) Meade-Fetherston-haugh, whose husband and son gave Uppark to the National Trust in 1954.

In the Red Drawing Room, firemen tore down the red flock wallpaper, first put up in c.1750 and papered over in 1851 or 1859. Because it was fixed to hessian and mounted on battens, rather than being stuck to the wall, it came away in huge strips and was hurled through the windows on to the lawn. Later that evening, at about 9.30pm, the pair of magnificent mid-eighteenth-century rococo carved and gilded pier-glasses, attributed to Matthias Lock, was unscrewed from the walls and, with great difficulty because the room was by now in flames, manoeuvred sideways through the windows. One of them was already on fire as it was manhandled to safety. The original bevelled glass, already cracked by the heat, was smashed to lighten the load.

It was no longer safe to enter some ground-floor rooms after about 6.30pm. The fire first broke through from above in the Stone Hall, the east (and original) entrance to the house. Here, National Trust staff could only look impotently through the glass doors as the room was rapidly ignited. Against the far wall, flanking the door into the Staircase Hall (a raging inferno for the last hour) stood the famous pair of scagliola-topped tables on English rococo supports. Two of the finest objects in the house, probably commissioned in Florence in 1750 by Sir Matthew Fetherstonhaugh, they were overlooked in the first phase of salvage due to their great weight and the fact that their bases were screwed to the panelled dado. Now, though only 15ft (4.5m) from the eastern steps, they were at the mercy of the fire.

The morning after the fire: flock wallpaper, torn down by firemen in the Red Drawing Room, is examined by Christopher Rowell and Mary Goodwin, then the National Trust's Adviser on Paper Conservation.

One of the bases was already burning when the ceiling collapsed at about 6.45pm, and engulfed the tables in rubble and burning debris. A falling beam smashed the left-hand table into eight pieces. It seemed at the time that both tables must have been totally destroyed.

Since all the rooms, with the single exception of the Little Parlour, were by now ablaze, the salvage operation became increasingly sporadic. As night drew in, and Uppark became a picturesque bonfire, the endless drone of the fire-pumps, the tangled hoses snaking around the house, the shouting of orders to the fire-crews and, above all, the crackling and spitting of blazing wood made up an unforgettable miscellany of images, sounds and smells. Occasionally, the collapse of a large piece of masonry or a wooden beam shook the ground as it fell in a shower of sparks. Members of the Meade-Fetherstonhaugh family, who had lost their home and almost their entire inheritance and who were at the forefront of the initial salvage effort, bravely confronted the awful reality of the destruction of their beloved Uppark.

At this stage, there was not much more to be done in terms of rescue. At 3am, National Trust staff were allowed for the first time into the north end of the building. In the company of the Chief Fire Officer, Martin Drury, then Historic Buildings Secretary, and Christopher Rowell looked through the door from the North Corridor into the Staircase Hall. Piled high with burning debris, it was an infernal scene. Miraculously, a length of seventeenth-century balustrade was still visible through the smoke on the first-floor landing, which had somehow not entirely collapsed. Much of the plasterwork was undamaged, but the seventeenth-century panelling below was destroyed.

Returning into the corridor, and turning right into the Servery, the party was able to review the state of the Dining Room. The Servery, and its stained-glass window by Humphry Repton, was undamaged. The scene beyond the double doors was encouraging. This panelled Dining Room, constructed by Repton for Sir Harry Fetherstonhaugh in *c.*1815, was hardly damaged (its ceiling had not yet fallen in). The gilt overmantel mirror, contemporary with Repton's work, was still in place. The question was, could it be safely retrieved? As a fireman entered through the window, he called out, 'Do you want the glass?' Concerned for his safety and wishing to avoid any delay as the ceiling might have collapsed at any moment, Martin Drury shouted, 'No'. The fireman smashed the glass with a crowbar and carried the frame to safety.

Leaving the building once again, the group toured the exterior for the last time that night. At the south-east corner, the Little Parlour was empty but still unscathed. Its eighteenth-century glass chandelier, hanging from crimson cords and tassels supplied in 1836, was swinging in the heat below the Neo-classical compartmented ceiling. A fireman was playing his hose into the room, attempting to reduce the possibility of flames igniting it. He was asked to divert his water jet away from the chandelier – a futile request in view of the subsequent collapse of the chimneystack high above, which crashed through the ceiling carrying the plasterwork, the chandelier and the Parlour floor into the Housekeeper's Room beneath. A last vignette that night was the spectacle of the Prince Regent's Bed, now beyond rescue, in the Tapestry Bedroom at the north-western extremity of the ground floor. Martin Drury and Christopher Rowell took what they were sure would be their last sight of Uppark's state bed and retired for the consolation of whisky and eggs and bacon, greedily consumed at 4am before three hours of fitful sleep.

Dawn revealed the full extent of the damage. The fire was still alight, but only smouldering by this time. An aerial photograph published in the *Portsmouth News* the following day, and then in several national newspapers, promoted the erroneous conclusion that Uppark had been 'gutted'. Gradually, it became evident that this was an exaggeration. The upper floors were indeed almost completely destroyed, but at ground-floor level, although all the ceilings had collapsed, much of the decorative plaster-work and woodwork had survived. The rooms were filled with wet smoking debris, but in the Saloon, where the paint and gilding of the walls and doorcases were remarkably untouched, the ormolu chandelier of *c.*1800 jutted out of the blackened rubbish, indicating the possibility of other survivals beneath. Here, and elsewhere, marble fireplaces had escaped damage. Although the Little Parlour had been destroyed in the course of the night, the Prince Regent's Bed still stood in the Tapestry Bedroom. There was no time to lose, as the ceiling looked precarious. At first, with shouted instructions from John Hart, one of the Trust's advisers on furniture conservation, firemen attempted to dismantle the bed. When they could not do it, John Hart and his assistant Gerard Bur joined them, lifted

Above: The scene facing Trust staff the day after the fire: (*right*) the balustrade of the Staircase Landing still miraculously in place, one of the few remnants of the main staircase to survive. Although damage was extensive and the ceilings had collapsed, much of the original decoration of the walls had been spared. In the Saloon (*left*) much of the painting and gilding survived almost undamaged, as did the marble chimneypieces. Within the rubble lay fragments of plaster, woodwork, and of the contents.

Left: The Little Parlour, a photograph taken in 1941. This was one of the rooms severely damaged in the fire.

off the canopy, unscrewed the frame and passed everything through the windows. Twenty minutes later, at about 10.30am, the ceiling collapsed.

Under the aegis of Sarah Staniforth, the Trust's adviser on paintings conservation, picture conservators from the Trust, the Royal Collection and in private practice had been working all night to consolidate canvases damaged by heat and water; this was done principally by laying down buckled paint and facing it with paper. A second shift relieved them at 8am. The damage sometimes looked more dramatic than it actually was: great streaks of blanched varnish caused by fire water were easily removed in subsequent studio treatment. By that evening, all the paintings had left Uppark for storage and for eventual conservation elsewhere. As they entered the van, their inventory numbers were ticked off and transport forms compiled. For reasons of security as well as conservation, furniture and other contents in a fit state to be moved were also transported within the following two days. With the television, radio and newspaper coverage, there was a very real risk of theft, but fortunately these precautions prevented it. Later, the building was fenced off and a perimeter alarm installed. Petworth House, another National Trust property ten miles to the east, became the repository for most of the salvaged contents. Here, at first, the Square Dining Room and Chapel were closed to the public 'for repair', but were in fact secretly filled with Uppark's now homeless collection; later, former servants' quarters in the Domestic Block were converted into longer-term safe storage. Subsequently, the defunct Battery House, once the site of electric generators that had powered both the house and the town, was converted into a temporary laying-out area where damaged Uppark contents were assessed before repair.

The day after the fire inaugurated many weeks of determined action to preserve what could be preserved of the fabric and contents of Uppark. The walls were still standing but they needed buttressing. Scaffolding could not be introduced without clearing the surrounding slag-heaps that filled the carcass of the building. For nearly five days until the fire was officially pronounced to be 'out', the fire brigade continued to 'damp down' the debris. Here and there small pockets of flame flared up and were extinguished. Despite this, it was possible to begin the excavation almost immediately. It was frustrating for those on site to be prevented from sifting through the sludge, but meanwhile there was more than enough to attend to. Thought had to be given not just to things but also to people. A home had to be found for the National Trust's resident custodians Brian and Jan Smith, whose flat and a lifetime's possessions were no more. The staff and outside conservators had to be equipped and fed. A system of regular, concise meetings was instigated to formulate a strategy for the rescue of damaged fragments of the building and its contents. Communication and co-ordination were essential, but conservators had to be given the time to proceed efficiently with the work in hand rather than to attend meetings.

Day-to-day management was split between Peter Pearce, then Managing Agent for Uppark (who dealt with general administration and had overall responsibility for the rescue) and Christopher Rowell (whose curatorship of the Uppark collection gave him a natural role in co-ordinating its conservation). A key figure, dubbed the Quartermaster, was John Sursham, previously the regional volunteers' co-ordinator, whose job was to procure anything that might be required, from voluntary help to portable telephones and food. He proved adept at obtaining huge numbers of dustbins, baker's trays and other mundane items that were to prove invaluable for the salvage operation. Three ballroom-sized marquees were pitched on the west lawn to enable sodden textiles to be slowly dried. Previously, at the instigation of Jane Mathews, then the Trust's adviser on textile conservation, the filthy and charred curtains had been interleaved with sheets of polythene. This dual process of keeping them moist, followed by natural drying in airy marquees avoided permanent staining.

Before the fire was officially extinguished, the fire brigade deemed it safe to dig out the several feet of debris in certain rooms. With watchers, armed with sirens to warn of any structural movement and stationed at a high level on the scaffolding, digging began. After most fires, even in important buildings, it had been the practice simply to cart away and dump the rubble, as, for example, after the 1980 fire at the National Trust's Nostell Priory, in Yorkshire. By contrast, after the fire at Hampton Court in 1986, investigation, recording and preservation of what was apparently rubbish had repaid considerable dividends.

At Uppark, teams of volunteers and staff under the supervision of the Trust's archaeological advisers and conservators systematically excavated the ruins. Each room (the sequence dictated by the condition of the surrounding walls) was separated into grid squares for the purpose of recording

Left: Rosalie Elwes, a National Trust volunteer, recording the departure of the paintings for studio repair. Essential emergency work by picture conservators had been completed within twenty-four hours of the fire.

Right: Once spotted in the rubble, interesting fragments were transferred to baker's trays marked with grid references, so that locations of the 'finds' could be recorded.

Left: Nearly 4,000 dustbins stored the residue of debris excavated within the ruins of the house. This was later sifted on a conveyor belt, which passed the rubble over a sieve.

the location of each 'find'. The grid consisted of a chequerboard of ropes stretched above the workers with letters and numbers designating each compartment. As interesting fragments emerged from the sludge (a piece of carved woodwork or plasterwork, sherds of glass and porcelain) they were placed in plastic trays labelled with the grid references. Thus it was possible to determine that broken glass found in the Staircase Hall belonged to the mid-eighteenth-century Gothick lantern previously hanging there. In this way, the glass was replaced to the exact profile of the original.

This initial sorting had to be carried out at speed, due to the urgent requirement to shore up the weakened walls of the building. The residue was shovelled into dustbins, also marked with grid references, to be sifted later on a conveyor belt which passed the debris over a mesh. The 3,860 dustbins on the east lawn beside the house became a potent symbol of the scale of the salvage operation. Plastic 'polytunnels' with scaffolding and plank shelving gradually filled up with great baulks of charred timber, trays of plaster fragments, carved decorative woodwork, window catches, door knobs, picture hooks, chimneypots and anything that looked promising. The clear principle was that nothing should be discarded lest vital clues for the possible repair of Uppark should be lost. As each room was cleared, the scaffolders moved in, and a honeycomb of supports began to rise. This steadily grew into a giant roofed structure of interlocking supports that was completed by November 1989.

Between August and November, as digging continued and discoveries were made in the rubble, conservators worked under considerable pressure,

Opposite: Excavating the ruins of the Red Drawing Room. Above the workers hangs a criss-cross network of ropes. Each square was numbered, and each fragment, or group of fragments, was labelled with the grid reference.

Right: This tray contains a remnant of the Saloon ceiling plasterwork.

Opposite: One of the three ball-room sized marquees erected on the west lawn to accommodate curtains and other textiles. The curtains, sodden with firewater, were first interleaved with polythene, then dried naturally in the marquees. This method, devised by Jane Mathews, then the Trust's Textile Conservation Adviser, avoided what would have been irreversible staining.

handling a huge and ever-increasing volume of fragile material. As Jane Mathews, who was working with a large team of textile conservators, put it: 'I'd never worked in field conditions before.' Because of the principle that nothing should be discarded, every piece of charred textile – however apparently insignificant – was carefully dusted with a small brush to remove acidic ash and residue, and each item was labelled and recorded. There were some dramatic moments, when casualties were carried from the battle-front of the house into what increasingly resembled a field hospital with white-coated conservators ministering quietly to their torn, scorched and bedraggled textiles. From the Red Drawing Room and Little Parlour, stretchered out on bread-trays, came the pathetic remains of four red silk chandelier tassels, supplied to Uppark in 1836. Already fragile in 1933 when they were taken down and repaired by Lady Meade-Fetherstonhaugh, they have once again been nursed back to life and now hang in their old positions, despite being crushed by several tons of rubble. Beneath the wreckage of the Red Drawing Room, against all reasonable expectations, lay the Axminster carpet of *c.*1800, a totally unexpected product of the optimism that had instigated the salvage operation. Hurriedly lifted and thrown over the Victorian Broadwood grand piano in a last-minute attempt to protect the (much less important) instrument from the fire, the piano had been incinerated, only its metal skeleton surviving within the folds of the carpet. Blackened, stained and damaged, the carpet responded well to emergency intensive care and was laid out to dry under canvas. It, too, has now returned to its old place.

With such encouragement, those working on site up to fourteen hours a day, seven days a week, began to feel that their efforts might not be in vain, and that Uppark might indeed have a future. It soon became possible to see how much plaster had been saved from the Saloon ceiling, how many lengths of gilt wallpaper fillet had emerged from the Red Drawing Room and so on. Most encouraging of all was the miraculous survival *in situ* of plasterwork, panelling, doors and chimneypieces. The decision to repair the house was taken two months after the fire, but those battling to save Uppark felt very quickly that this would be the likely outcome, and worked all the harder with this hope in mind. As they worked, the pieces of the jigsaw were increasing day by day, and an intense camaraderie developed. Everyone concerned looks back to that time as a period of single-minded hard labour. They remember how exhausted they were at night (and in the morning before another long day) but they also recall the 'blitz' spirit of working together for something worthwhile. At first, wartime analogies extended even to the food, which was not only reminiscent of 1940s deprivation but also of the 'Monty Python' menu of 'spam, spam, spam or spam'. Mercifully, cheese or spam sandwiches and Mars bars soon gave way to more digestible alternatives.

Just as they had rallied to the emergency call, so the conservators in private practice, many with a long history of working on Trust buildings and collections, continued to work day after day with no thought of remuneration. No one waited for an order to come through before beginning work, and the Trust's administrative staff had to ensure much later that nobody was out of pocket due to this generosity and selfless dedication. In the rescue and subsequent repair of Uppark the Trust's conservation service came of age.

As the rooms were gradually cleared, not only did the scaffolding enabling emergency repairs to take place (only one chimneystack had to be pulled down) begin to rise, but also the recording of the damaged interior was instituted. With the help of the National Monuments Record, the Trust's archaeological department surveyed the structure both as a possible preliminary to reconstruction and as an historical record. This was later supplemented by photogrammetry (precision photography to scale), which allowed the data to be incorporated on computer as an essential basis for architects' computer-assisted drawings. Computers were also brought in by the English Heritage Archaeological Excavation Team that had pioneered their technique after the 1986 Hampton Court fire. In early November they joined National Trust rescuers and began the process of transferring manual records of over 12,000 finds on to their 'Delilah' computer programme. This was of considerable benefit, but its efficacy was qualified by the understandable misidentification of objects by inexperienced recording staff. Later, when the repairs were under way, only expert manual sorting would reveal how many eighteenth-century metal curtain cloakpins or window catches had survived, because they had been filed on the computer as 'miscellaneous metalwork'. As ever, automation proved not to be a panacea.

Research was also already in progress to establish the extent of pre-fire records that could serve to inform the possible renaissance of Uppark. Fortunately, Uppark had been extensively photographed since the late nineteenth century. The first *Country Life* article was illustrated in 1910, and family albums produced even earlier images. As well as the National Trust photographic archive, photographs were sent in by visitors, scholars, craftsmen and builders in response to the Trust's appeal for help. Later, the appeal became more specialised as the lacunae became more apparent. A snapshot of a pet owl perching on the shoulder of the Uppark

Custodian's niece, for instance, proved to be the only evidence for the design of the attic kitchen in the Custodian's flat. On the first floor, Meade-Fetherstonhaugh family photographs solved the confusion about wallpaper colours and chimneypieces.

The principal rooms on the ground floor were, hardly surprisingly, more comprehensively recorded. There were also National Trust surveys of pictures and, more importantly, of picture and mirror frames. The latter proved to be of fundamental significance for the recarving of the destroyed base sections of one of the Red Drawing Room pier-glasses. There was also a series of general views of each room. None the less, there were gaps (which could usually be filled by resort to fragments recovered after the fire, or by comparative research), and some photographs were endlessly magnified and pored over in an endeavour to make sense of some missing detail. Needless to say, there is now a mandatory policy of architectural photography that, when completed, will provide a comprehensive record of all the Trust's buildings and collections.

From the first puff of smoke, Uppark's demise had been captured on film by amateurs and professionals. Thousands of photographs, hundreds of hours of film and tape recordings, as well as rooms full of documents, provide an exceptional opportunity for future study of what was done. Thanks to the generosity of Sun Alliance, which, as the Sun Fire Office, first insured Uppark in 1753, visitors see an introductory exhibition which draws upon this voluminous material. The educational potential is at least one silver lining to the catastrophe of 1989.

In 1753 Sir Matthew Fetherstonhaugh insured Uppark with the Sun Fire Office (see page 45). As immediate proof of insurance, company badges were affixed to buildings and were also worn, in silver or silver-gilt, by company firemen. This lead wall plaque was presumably supplied to Uppark in 1753.

DEMOLISH IT!

MP's call after Uppark inferno

By GILL BAKER

PORTSMOUTH M.P. David Martin today called for the fire-ravaged Uppark House to be demolished.

Mr. Martin, member for Portsmouth South, wants the Downland site of the historic mansion at South Harting, on the Hampshire/West Sussex border, returned to nature.

He believes approval to build the house would never have been given in the present day because of pressure to protect green-field sites.

Fire gutted the important 17th-Century National Trust house a week ago.

Mr. Martin said: "Imagine attempting to get planning permission for building a house in such a position today.

"The very same great people supporting the National Trust and similar bodies wanting to re-

"We can pull it down, maintain it as a ruin, or rebuild it.

"Most workers on site are hoping there will be a possibility we can rebuild. A decision still has to be made, but it will not be for a few weeks."

She said demolition was "unlikely."

Meanwhile a second smaller fire broke out in a charred beam at the house yesterday morning, a week after the initial blaze.

■ South Harting villager Mr. Roger Williamson has claimed the effects of the fire could have been lessened.

He said: "Ever since the house was built it has been known in the

Fire at Uppark

From Mr David Martin, MP for Portsmouth South (Conservative)

Sir, The expressed intent to restore the fire-ruined Uppark House in Sussex surprises me. In these days of outrage at development of green-field sites, let alone a prominent one on a Sussex Downs hilltop, here is an ideal opportunity to demolish it altogether and return the site to nature.

Imagine attempting to get planning permission for building such a house (or rather museum business premises) in such a position today! The very same great and good people supporting the National Trust and similar bodies wanting to restore it would be leading petitions, dismayed letters to MPs etc., to preserve such an area of high landscape value and unique habitat for something or other from being vandalised by developers.

In their assaults on vast acres of our countryside, were the yuppies of the 17th century so very different? Why should we allow time to confer legitimacy on *their* depredations?

Yours truly,
DAVID MARTIN,
House of Commons.

Uppark to be restored

Uppark House, the historic Harting mansion destroyed by fire, will be restored to its former glory, the National Trust has announced.

The news was welcomed by local people and those working on the site salvaging the charred contents.

At the height of the blaze more than 150 firemen were at the 17th century house on the West Sussex/Hampshire border.

Nearly all the contents

of the ground floor were saved by the prompt action of firemen and volunteers but the entire contents were lost from the private apartments above.

National Trust chiefs met this week to decide the future of the house and had three options to consider: whether to restore it, demolish it or retain it as a ruined monument.

After a lengthy meeting they agreed the house would be restored to its appearance before the fire with efforts being made to use as much of the original fabrication and decoration as possible.

National Trust Director General Mr. Angus Stirling said: "Far more of Uppark and its contents survive than have been lost. There is a real phoenix, not a false one, to be raised from the ashes. It would be faint-hearted indeed of the trust not to face up to the challenge of what will be the greatest single building conservation project the trust has ever undertaken."

Acting site manager Miss Sara Braune said: "It is wonderful news. Everyone is delighted."

The cost of restoration,

which could be as much as £20m. and take ten years, is fully covered by insurance.

Salvage work is expected to continue for another two to three months and foundations are now being dug ready to construct a huge temporary roof over the structure to protect it from the elements.

Ninety four-year-old Harting resident Mrs. Phyllis Hosking said: "Whether one agrees with it or not, they could not do anything else because the insurance was for restoration. So if the National Trust did not accept that offer the money would be lost. That is how the National Trust's hands are bound. They either have to play by the rules or lose the money."

Chairman of Harting Parish Council Capt. Brian Evans said: "I am very pleased it is to be restored. I think the rebuilding project will draw many interesting people into the area and it will be

fascinating to see the place restored so all the furniture and other items can be housed in the surroundings they were used to before."

Uppark House, which, in August, was gutted by fire. Photo. sales no. 2028-7

UPPARK PHOENIX VOTE BRINGS JOY

£20m works may take ten years

By GILL BAKER and MIKE MORTON

SALVAGE workers and residents today welcomed the news that Uppark, the historic mansion destroyed by fire, will be restored to its former glory by the National Trust.

The cost of restoration, which could be as much as £20m. and take ten years, is fully covered by insurance.

Trust executives announced their decision after spending most of the day discussing options for the future of the mansion at Harting.

"There is a real phoenix, not a false one, to be raised from the ashes. It would be faint-hearted indeed of the trust not to face up to the challenge of what will be the greatest single building conservation project the trust has ever undertaken."

Acting site manager Miss Sara Braune said: "It is wonderful news. Everyone is delighted."

Salvage work is expected to continue for another two to three months and foundations are now being dug ready to construct a huge temporary roof over the structure to protect it from the

---

MANSION WILL RISE AGAIN

UPPARK, the 17th century Sussex manor house destroyed by fire, is to undergo a complete restoration.

Flashback — after the blaze

2: The Decision to Restore

WHILE THE HOUSE was still burning, a lengthy debate on its future began. Should Uppark be restored or demolished, provided with a new interior, or the shell stabilised as a ruin? In a press release issued immediately after the fire Martin Drury declared: 'We shall reconstruct Uppark if we can, although it is too soon to know if this is possible.' Nearly all the contents of the public rooms had been salvaged, thanks to the heroic efforts of the rescuers, and on 13 September 1989 David Sekers announced: 'We feel that enough survives to justify total restoration.' Christopher Rowell also pointed out that whereas at first the house was thought to be gutted, 'on closer inspection' it was found that, though the fire had destroyed the attic and first floor, it had consumed only part of the ground floor and very little of the basement. His view confirmed that 'the omens are good and that the house can rise from the ashes.'

These statements sparked off a debate in the newspapers. A correspondent wrote to *The Times* on 18 September 1989: 'The result of such misguided activity will be very largely a fake; a very skilful fake, I have no doubt, but a fake (or if you prefer it a "reproduction antique") none the less. What will be the point of this? Those visiting Uppark in the future would know it was a copy of the original; would the public therefore go to see it anymore?' (The answer to this question is that when the house reopened in the summer of 1995 over 60,000 visitors came to see it in the first five months – double the annual total before the fire.)

Several argued that the site should be 'returned to nature', and airily claimed that the 'rescued furniture and paintings etc. can easily be found worthy homes elsewhere'. The demolition argument was most memorably put by Mr David Martin, the Conservative MP for Portsmouth South, in a letter to *The Times* on 6 September 1989:

Sir,
The expressed intent to restore the fire-ruined Uppark House in Sussex surprises me. In these days of outrage at development of green-field sites, let alone a prominent one on a Sussex Downs hilltop, here is an ideal opportunity to demolish it altogether and return the site to nature.

Imagine attempting to get planning permission for building such a house

The Uppark fire was extensively covered in the press, leading to a debate about the house's future.

(or rather museum business premises) in such a position today! The very same great and good people supporting the National Trust and similar bodies wanting to restore it would be leading petitions, dismayed letters to MPs etc., to preserve such an area of high landscape value and unique habitat for something or other from being vandalised by developers.

In their assaults on vast acres of our countryside, were the yuppies of the 17th century so very different? Why should we allow time to confer legitimacy on *their* depredations?

Yours truly,

DAVID MARTIN,

House of Commons.

This evoked a certain amount of derision in the local press, being generally denounced as 'arrogant nonsense', and provoking the SDP leader of the opposition on the Hampshire County Council, Mike Hancock, to call him 'the biggest philistine since Goliath'. He added: 'Obviously Mr Martin has neither feeling for, nor knowledge of, history.'

Deyan Sudjic, in an article in the now-defunct *Sunday Correspondent* on 17 September 1989, expressed the true Modernist spirit: '...it won't actually *be* Uppark, no matter how skilful the work of the 20th-century craftsmen who seek to recreate it. What tourists come to see will, in fact, be a replica, one which could be said to diminish those fragments which actually are authentic...' He continued: 'It [Uppark] will become a monument to the 20th century's inability to accept the consequences of catastrophe.' (Surely, some of the noblest aspirations of twentieth-century civilisation have been its attempts to come to terms with catastrophe: Lutyens's Cenotaph and war cemeteries of the First World War, for instance, or the reconstruction of Warsaw and St Petersburg after the Second World War.) A couple of faint-hearted journalists in the *Guardian* and *Independent* also argued that it would in effect be morally wrong to attempt a facsimile restoration. 'A new Uppark can never be the same as *the* Uppark...' And Anna Pavord, for instance, recommended a plain modern interior within the seventeenth-century shell.

Most commentators, however, urged that Uppark should be restored. On 7 September 1989, in the *Daily Telegraph*, Mark Bence-Jones pointed out robustly that the Trust's 'credibility as a guardian of the Nation's Heritage' depended upon its response to the Uppark fire. To use the insurance money for any purpose other than for rebuilding would, he stated, be a form of alienation and a betrayal of the donors' intentions in handing over the house in 1954 for permanent preservation. Dan Cruikshank in *Country Life*, on 18 January 1990, recommended rebuilding as the wisest course. Not only would a restored interior be the most 'suitable setting for the contents', but also the reconstruction could form a model demonstration of the correct use of traditional materials and decorative techniques.

'With this work completed, the house could be more popular than ever – since together with "before and after" photographs, it would be a dramatic testament to the committed recreation of a national monument.' Others made the point that the rebuilding would provide an unequalled opportunity to foster skills in historic preservation 'where experts can demonstrate their knowledge and craftsmen could be trained.'

Professor Andor Gomme (Professor of Architectural History at the University of Keele) reinforced the argument for restoration in a letter to the *Independent* on 3 October 1989:

Sir: Uppark is the third great house which the National Trust has lost through fire since the last war. Both Coleshill (burnt in 1953) and Dunsland (1967) were subsequently entirely destroyed – decisions which have been deeply deplored ever since. [In fact, Coleshill burnt before the estate came to the Trust.] Uppark is a house of comparable importance and value, and its full restoration is essential.

Anna Pavord's proposal … that the interior should be rebuilt as 'a series of simple, clean, well-designed rooms' for the display of the contents saved from the fire ignores the fact that the furniture and paintings at Uppark were either designed or collected by the Fetherstonhaugh family over numerous generations especially for the rooms in which they lived. Shorn of these surroundings the furnishings would be just another museum collection...

Had Germany taken the 'purist' line after the war, we should be without the wonders of Bruchsal and the Residenz at Würzburg, and the great churches of Nürnberg would look like the clean well-designed – but totally anaemic – interiors of those in Kassel and Stuttgart. Where, as appears to be the case at Uppark, it is physically possible to make an accurate restoration of a great building, it should be made and not jeered at as a creation of a theme park of misnamed pastiche.

This debate has to be seen in the context of a philosophy of restoration which has developed in Britain since the later nineteenth century, and is still much influenced by the writings and opinions of those larger-than-life Victorian defenders of old buildings John Ruskin (1819–1900) and William Morris (1834–98). Ruskin was horrified by the cavalier 'restoration' and drastic reconstruction of medieval churches in England and on the Continent by Gothic architects such as Sir George Gilbert Scott (1811–78) or Viollet-le-duc (1814–79), who frequently removed later features of interest and replaced them with their own, often hypothetical, reconstructions of what might have been. Ruskin also had inveighed against 'desecration' and argued that old buildings should be valued in themselves, but not 'improved'. His pupil William Morris developed this theory, arguing that old buildings should be merely patched in the gentlest possible way, and that all such repairs should be distinctive so that the viewer would not be deceived into thinking that the new work was old. In theory, if carried to its logical extreme, this philosophy could lead to peculiar visual results with, for example, a corroded window mullion being

Alfriston Clergy House, Sussex, was the Trust's first historic building, bought for £10 in 1896, the year after the Trust was founded. Virtually in ruins (*left*), it was restored with the advice of the Society for the Protection of Ancient Buildings.

replaced in a different material rather than matching its neighbour in stone. In practice, it inspired some of the most beautiful and evocative restorations ever carried out in England: old churches in Herefordshire or Sussex, for example, where Georgian box pews and lime plaster ceilings were left alongside Gothic work, or houses like Morris's own Kelmscott, in Oxfordshire, or Haddon Hall, in Derbyshire, not to mention much that the National Trust itself has achieved, including the repair of many of its earliest acquisitions like the Clergy House at Alfriston, in East Sussex, or vernacular villages such as Lacock, in Wiltshire, and West Wycombe, in Buckinghamshire.

In order to promote the appropriate repair of old buildings, William Morris founded the still flourishing Society for the Protection of Ancient Buildings (SPAB) in 1877. Morris's choice of the word protection rather than preservation is significant. His aim was to protect buildings from unsuitable restoration and alterations, as much as from demolition, ruin and decay. What might be called the SPAB approach to historic buildings has evolved principally with medieval and vernacular buildings in mind, where the ancient structure itself has considerable archaeological interest. Much of the visual appeal of such buildings derives from the inimitable texture, techniques, colours of natural materials, hand-craftsmanship and time-worn finishes. It is more difficult to apply the same principles to Victorian buildings with their hard, cast or moulded industrial materials and machine methods, or even to Georgian buildings, where at least as much of the aesthetic impact derives from the architect's design – three-dimensional spaces, symmetry, proportion and well-deployed classical ornament – as from the execution by craftsmen or the 'patina of history'.

This purist approach to the restoration of old buildings has been further complicated since the mid-twentieth century by the intellectual legacy of architectural Modernism. The Modern Movement decisively rejected the

use of traditional techniques and materials or the inclusion of architectural ornament in favour of uncompromisingly severe buildings with unencumbered lines and 'new' materials such as concrete, steel and plate glass. Modernism has affected the way in which many people, especially those trained in schools of architecture, look at historic buildings. In general, Modern Movement theory was antipathetical towards old buildings; it was thought that they had no place in the Brave New World. A 'modern industrial society' (whatever that might be) required buildings of a type totally different from anything hitherto enjoyed by the human race. Le Corbusier, for instance, whose ideas had an enormous impact after the Second World War, produced an 'ideal' plan for the complete demolition of central Paris and its reconstruction on a 'rational' grid with evenly spaced tower blocks. The influence of this type of thought is visible in the planning and reconstruction of most English towns and cities in the 1960s and is still a force in contemporary architectural doctrine, even if not a very potent one.

Although the Modern Movement is no longer dominant, its influence lingers, colouring attitudes towards historic buildings and traditional craftsmanship in Britain. It manifests itself as a subliminal Puritanism which regards any sort of historicist decoration or the use of traditional materials as 'pastiche' or 'fake'. Its proponents have little sympathy with the concept of scholarly or accurate restoration of historic buildings. They tend to regard any form of copying as morally wrong. If something old is damaged or destroyed, they consider that it should not be repaired or copied, but swept away and replaced with something in the 'style of our time' or 'good new design', by which they mean Modern architecture. The Royal Institute of British Architects (RIBA), the professional mouthpiece of 25,000 practising architects, still gives regular expression to these views. The *RIBA Journal*, for instance, described the completed Uppark restoration as 'the

2 Willow Road in Hampstead, the house built and lived in by the modernist architect, Ernö Goldfinger, and acquired by the National Trust in 1994. In order to build the house in 1937, Goldfinger demolished a row of eighteenth-century cottages (*left*) despite a public outcry.

equivalent of a Wimpey house but for its sadly forced, intellectualised veneer'.

It is the fond belief of many that when in the past good old buildings were damaged by fire the owners always demolished them and commissioned the 'best architects of the day' to build new and even better houses than the ones they had lost. Sometimes they did, but often they did not. There is, in fact, a long and serious tradition of copying and restoring historic buildings in Europe. (In Japan many historic buildings, being of timber, are rebuilt in replica at regular intervals, especially some of the 'old' Shinto temples: the Ise Shrine, near Kyoto, for instance, is reconstructed every twenty years). When Doncaster parish church burnt down in 1853, Sir Giles Gilbert Scott rebuilt it partly as a reproduction of what had been there before the fire. Following the gutting of the Winter Palace in St Petersburg in the 1830s the interior was reinstated as it had been on the evidence of detailed watercolours. This was also the case with the Fenice theatre in Venice (alas, burnt again in 1996). Likewise, after the Private Dining Room at Windsor Castle was destroyed by fire in 1853, Anthony Salvin (1799–1881) reconstructed it exactly according to Jeffry Wyatville's 1828 designs.

Many fire-damaged country houses in Britain have been restored over the past two centuries. When Thomas Archer's Bramham Park, in Yorkshire, was gutted in 1828, the Lane-Fox family did not demolish the shell and commission a good modern architect to design a new house; they simply reroofed it. After Duncombe Park (also in Yorkshire) burnt in 1879, Lord Feversham called in William Young (architect of the War Office in London) to reinstate it in the spirit of the original. When fire demolished the central block at Stourhead, in Wiltshire, in 1902, the Hoare family employed Aston and Dorian Webb to undertake repairs, and most of the rooms are now reasonable copies of their predecessors. The same happened at Monzie Castle, in Perthshire, in 1908 and in 1911 at Sledmere, in Yorkshire, where Joseph Rose's destroyed plasterwork was recreated by George Jackson & Sons, the firm which was to be awarded the Uppark plastering contract. At Hagley, in Worcestershire, a remarkably skilful restoration of the main rooms was carried out after a fire in 1925, including copying damaged rococo ceilings and thereby foreshadowing the Uppark project.

Particularly successful restorations since the Second World War have included the Wyatt Dining Room at Heveningham Hall, in Suffolk, after a fire in 1949, and the rebuilding of the dome at Castle Howard, in Yorkshire, following its destruction in 1940. Many restorations and reinstatements of old houses after fires have been carried out so unobtrusively that many people do not realise what has happened. The evidence suggests that most owners have taken a pragmatic decision about whether to restore or to replace their houses.

The theory that architects and artists never copied in the past is not supported by the evidence. Numerous examples can be quoted. Some of the seemingly medieval quadrangles at Oxford date from the seventeenth or even eighteenth centuries. Half the symmetrical Elizabethan façade of Stonyhurst, in Lancashire, dates from 1590 and half from the 1830s. At Westminster Abbey the late fourteenth-century nave is an exact copy of the mid-thirteenth-century choir, and Hawksmoor's eighteenth-century towers continue the style of the Perpendicular west front. Sir William Chambers's Georgian front of Somerset House facing the Strand is a copy of John Webb's demolished river front. Much of the 'Elizabethan' exterior of Longford Castle, in Wiltshire, is in fact a Victorian reconstruction by Anthony Salvin. And this is just to mention a handful of representative examples from different centuries.

Something of this historical background needs to be borne in mind when considering the arguments aired in the press, and elsewhere, by different parties regarding the 'correct' way to treat Uppark after the fire. Many offered advice in early September 1989, before the true extent of damage was known. The SPAB, for example, urged that if the interior had been gutted 'no attempt should be made to create a lifeless replica of the eighteenth-century rooms.' Instead, it suggested, the shell should be con- solidated, a roof added and the internal spaces reconstructed as a museum of the National Trust contents. This work should be done to 'the highest standards of today and could result in beautiful and memorable rooms'. This view was moderated once the true extent of the damage was clearer. The SPAB expanded its philosophy of conservation as it applied to Uppark in an article by its secretary, Philip Venning, in its 1989 autumn newsletter. It is worth discussing, as it is the best expression of a particular and in- fluential attitude towards restoration, and an honest attempt to grapple with the philosophical questions raised by the arguments in favour of repair versus restoration.

The basic question at Uppark was the extent to which the destroyed parts of the decorative interior should be replaced in replica, if at all. The SPAB was prominent among those urging the National Trust not to commit itself to total restoration of the house. Philip Venning's article acknowledged that the Trust had, even before the fire was extinguished, mobilised 'the most impressive post-disaster operation seen in this country'. It also recognised that 95 per cent of the contents of the ground-floor rooms had been saved and praised the efficiency with which archaeologists, conservators and other specialists had begun the stabilisation of the shell, and the salvage and 'first-aid' conservation of the remnants. Whereas the upper part of the house, the home of the Meade-Fetherstonhaugh family, and its contents had been totally obliterated, it described the picture at basement and ground-floor level as 'more mixed'. 'The Saloon, less its decorative ceiling, has come off best of all and survives in most of its beauty.

The Little Parlour: (*above*) looking north-east in 1941; (*below*) the carved wooden fireplace of the late 1740s, damaged by the fire when the room's ceiling and floor were carried into the basement as a result of the collapse of the chimney-stack.

The Little Parlour
looking south-west after
the fire. The ceiling and
floor have collapsed, but
the walls and woodwork
are relatively unscathed.

By contrast the stairs have vanished, and the Dining Room is a tragic
remnant. [This proved over-pessimistic]. Other rooms vary in the extent of
damage.'

Adherents of the SPAB standpoint sincerely believed that a copy of any
work of art is, to quote from the same article, 'at best a lifeless imitation'
and that a modern reproduction is not an adequate substitute for a great
work of art which has been lost in a fire. 'No restorer, however clever, can
put back the missing ingredient at Uppark – 250 years of historic creativity
and use.' This assertion slightly begs the question. A house is not an auto-
graph work of art like a great painting: it is the joint result of many hands –
plasterers, joiners, masons, carvers, decorators and gilders – interpreting
and executing the concept of the architect, as well as a composite of alterations and adjustments made since completion. It is difficult to argue that
a twentieth-century copy of an eighteenth-century ceiling is different in

The accuracy of Uppark's restoration depended upon precise recording of the structure after the fire. Here, a member of the architectural staff works on a drawing of the north front.

kind from, say, a Victorian renewal of an eighteenth-century red flock paper. In a slowly evolving and changing entity like a country house, later decoration and restoration work is surely as much part of the history of the building as anything that went before.

The purists argued that the philosophical problem was greatest in the rooms where only some of the original workmanship survived. How far should damaged rooms be totally restored? How far should the salvaged fragments of plaster, joinery, carving and metalwork be reinstated, or simply used as patterns to copy? Many doubted whether it was technically feasible to incorporate the salvaged fragments in the restoration. Others took the more straightforward view that Uppark presented not a philosophical but a practical problem. If it was technically possible to restore the house, then it should be done.

Since the 1970s there had been a number of competent restorations of fire-damaged interiors: Inveraray Castle, in Argyllshire, by Ian Lindsay & Partners; the Music Room at Brighton Pavilion, by Brighton Corporation; three rooms on the *piano nobile* at Nostell Priory by the National Trust; the library at Cullen, in Banffshire, by Kit Martin; and the King's State Apartments at Hampton Court by the Historic Royal Palaces Agency. Out of these disasters has evolved a whole new armoury of skills and methods. It could be argued that accurate, scholarly restoration of historic buildings in Britain is a quintessentially late twentieth-century architectural phenomenon, drawing as it does on thorough archival research, modern recording techniques and the application of developed archaeological practice.

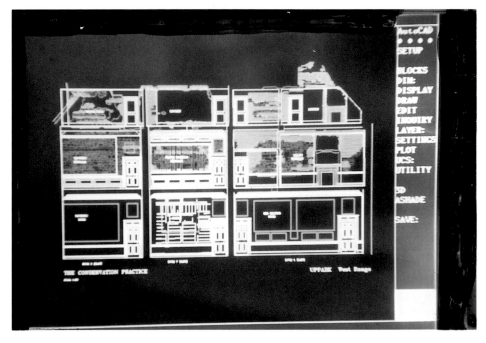

Measured elevations were worked up by computer to produce accurate computer-aided drawings (CAD).

Detailed photographic and photogrammetric records and computer-aided drawings (CAD) have made possible a degree of speed and accuracy in restoration work never before attainable. The use of such 'high-tech' resources, as well as new scholarly disciplines, is just as valid and distinctive an expression of the twentieth century as steel and concrete construction, float glass or any other technological advance.

Technology is only a means to an end, however, and not an end in itself. Craftsmanship still remains paramount, although modern techniques of recording and surveying buildings are useful ingredients in successful architectural restoration. Regrettably, such techniques were not available when the gutted Wren churches in the City of London or the Bath Assembly Rooms were reconstructed after the blitz. A comparison between these early post-war restorations and those at Cullen or Hampton Court more recently shows the advances in architectural restoration in the last fifty years. The National Trust's experience of restoring Nostell after the fire in 1980 and the lessons learned there were to prove useful at Uppark. In no respect could the Nostell disaster be called a 'dress rehearsal', but it had shown what could be done to resurrect gutted and partially damaged Georgian rooms and that the high quality of traditional craftsmanship required by such work was still available. The differences at Uppark, however, were many; not least, there was a difference of scale, with eight state-rooms requiring extensive restoration, as well as the repairs to the fabric and the reconstruction of the residential upper floors.

In a memorandum of 19 September 1989, intended as guidance to the

Executive Committee, the Trust's Director-General, Angus Stirling, outlined the three options facing the Trust – demolition of the shell, preservation of the ruin and restoration – all of which had found their passionate advocates in the correspondence, both public and private, following the fire. While demolition would follow the precedent of Coleshill, the memorandum pointed out that there were other historic sites, such as Clumber Park, in Nottinghamshire, where the main house had been destroyed, leaving only outbuildings as a reminder of greater days. Whereas there might be a 'superficial attraction' in returning the Sussex Down to its natural state, the stonework and architectural detail of the exterior constituted a monument which it would arguably be a vandalistic act to destroy. Moreover, in the light of the providential rescue of the contents, demolition would be 'unwise' and 'irresponsible'. While taking account of the strong feeling expressed that the soul of Uppark had been destroyed, the memorandum argued that to preserve the house as a ruin would forfeit the beauty and historic traditions that still resided within its walls. Finally, it stated that the survival of most of the contents and the insurance position favoured restoration and hoped that the Committee would feel able to decide upon this course.

On 4 October 1989 the National Trust's Executive Committee, having fully considered the options, decided to restore Uppark to its appearance of 'the day before the fire'. This decision, supported by the majority of committee members with only two voting against it, was based on practicalities rather than abstract philosophical concepts. In the first place, the building was far from being a write-off: the shell, substantial parts of the ground-floor rooms (about 70 per cent of the original fabric, including 90 per cent of metalwork and 65 per cent of the textiles) and all the basement remained. Thanks to the corset of scaffolding which surrounded the building (for the benefit of the roof workers) the outer walls were still stable. Uppark is a Grade I Listed Building and English Heritage would simply not have consented to its total demolition. Retention as a ruin was not practical. The best way to preserve a shell, especially one built of brick and lime mortar in England (where it rains) is to protect it with a roof so that only the exterior walls get wet. To have created a new interior within the preserved shell would have involved the destruction of the substantial parts of the surviving part of the ground-floor interior and would have provided an anachronistic setting for the collection. Again, the grant of Listed Building Consent would not have been forthcoming from English Heritage for such a course.

Second, the building was comprehensively insured for total reinstatement by a syndicate led by Sun Alliance. The insurance money could only be used for the rebuilding and repair of Uppark and not for any other purpose. Third, 95 per cent of the contents of the state-rooms – pictures, furniture, ceramics, carpets, books and so forth – had been rescued during

A record of Sir Matthew's insurance of Uppark. He chose the Sun Fire Office, founded in 1710 and incorporated in the present Royal Sun Alliance Insurance Company in 1959. Sun Alliance was the principal insurer of the building at the time of the fire and continues to insure Uppark.

the fire and could be put back in their original positions. The National Trust, a champion of the historically authentic, non-museum display of works of art, considered it important that the contents, which had been designed or purchased specifically for the house by two generations of discerning Georgian collectors, should be seen again in their natural surroundings. Partial restoration of the interior would have greatly reduced its quality as a setting for the eighteenth-century collection. Each part of Uppark contributed to a greater whole. Wilfully to have omitted the destroyed parts of the original architecture on doctrinaire philosophical grounds would have turned the house into a didactic archaeological display. What would have been gained, for instance, by giving the Saloon a plain ceiling or leaving the north wall of the Dining Room as bare brickwork, when the rest of these rooms and their furniture, pictures and other fixtures and fittings had largely survived or were capable of repair? Finally, Uppark was well-documented, with a detailed photographic record of the main rooms, as well as thousands of fragments retrieved after the fire, furnishing evidence for their full reinstatement. As we have seen, the rescue, sieving and recording of nearly 4,000 dustbins had provided a basic catalogue of all the salvaged material, from primary floor joists to small nails. In October 1989 the National Trust had also commissioned a complete photogrammetric survey of the surviving structure. As a result of this, there were very few details of the building which were not known; the evidence was available for an absolutely accurate reconstruction of Uppark, incorporating everything that had survived the fire.

Above all, the National Trust considered it vital that Uppark should have a continued life. The fire had been a major disaster but it need not be terminal. The Trust took heart from the Latin motto on a Victorian Fether-stonhaugh hatchment: *Non Omnis Moriar* (I shall not wholly die). Much more of the house had survived than had originally been thought. The main rooms were capable of skilful repair and this would not, in the Trust's view, be pastiche. If philosophical quibbles were put aside and common sense allowed to prevail, all the problems presented by reinstatement could be resolved.

The brief prepared by the National Trust for the architect embodied these two key principles: that the house was to be rebuilt to match its appearance of the day before the fire and that the reconstruction should incorporate conserved remnants wherever possible, but subject to strict commercial scrutiny. The latter was a requirement of the Trust's insurers, who insisted on the most economical approach. Their Loss Adjusters were adamant that original components should only be reinstated where it could be shown that it was no more expensive to do so than to make a replacement of equivalent quality. In the event it proved consistently cheaper to reuse old work wherever practicable rather than to copy, even allowing for the cost of initial repair.

There still remained, however, much to settle. If the house was to be reinstated to its condition on the day before the fire, did this mean putting back out-of-date cast-iron radiators? The Trust's response was that the general principle applied to the architecture and decoration but that all services would be modernised and the most advanced heating systems, humidity control, fire detection and security technology would be discreetly introduced, just as they had been in other National Trust houses as part of the major overhaul of the fabric: for instance, at Waddesdon Manor, in Buckinghamshire, or Ham House, in Surrey, where the whole of the domestic services had just been renewed.

Debate continued about the details of restoration in each room. The SPAB and architectural historians, such as Dan Cruikshank of the Georgian Group, urged that all the salvaged fragments should be incorporated and not just used as models to copy. Where substantial amounts of original fabric remained in particular rooms, careful repair and 'judicious replacement of lacunae' were essential in order to retain the integrity of the whole. Once it had become clear how much had escaped the conflagration, the only real difference of opinion remaining between the SPAB and the National Trust was the scale of some of the 'lacunae' to be replaced. The

The Staircase Hall: (*right*) as the epicentre of the fire, little survived of the seventeenth-century staircase and the panelling in the lower hall. Although the ceiling collapsed, the mid eighteenth-century plasterwork of the walls above survived almost intact; (*left*) the staircase had to be totally rebuilt, incorporating a few sections of the original. The floorboards remarkably survived in large part. The redecoration of the Hall is based on documentary and paint analysis evidence of an early nineteenth-century pink and white scheme (see p.113).

National Trust felt that the main staircase, which had been almost destroyed in the fire, should be reinstated to its original design so as to preserve the unity and sequence of the ground-floor rooms. The SPAB still considered that the destruction here provided an opportunity for a 'really good and inventive architect' to show what could be done. 'In the case of the stair well, the SPAB holds the view that the resulting void must be filled by new design. To achieve this satisfactorily the architect must exercise aesthetic judgement within an overall philosophical framework ... we respect the craftsmanship of the past by adding the best of our day.' John Bonython, an architect and a Georgian enthusiast had no truck with that, and in a letter to *Country Life* in 1989 retorted that 'the only staircase design that can make sense at Uppark is the original one.'

This was the line taken by the Trust, given that it was the consistent appearance of the sequence of ground-floor rooms that counted most. The replacement of the destroyed or damaged elements of the oak staircase and of the decorative plaster ceilings was not that different from the restoration of holes in a large canvas, and ensured that the total *mise-en-scène* could still be 'read' as a visual entity. Angus Stirling expressed the spirit behind the restoration when he announced the Trust's decision to rebuild: 'Far more of Uppark and its contents survive than have been lost ... It would be fainthearted not to face up to the challenge of what will be the greatest single building conservation project the Trust has ever undertaken.'

Marcus Binney, the President of SAVE Britain's Heritage, summed up the views of most of those professionally involved in the care of historic buildings and their collections in an article, provocatively entitled 'Purists cheated by the Phoenix,' in *The Times* of 8 October 1989: 'The Trust has decided rightly and has won the gratitude of all who cherish Britain's architectural heritage.' He wrote enthusiastically about what had survived:

Uppark's three main façades, commanding a matchless view across the South Downs, are largely intact except for the pediment. Brickwork and stonework are miraculously unscorched. Much of the 18th century window glass survived.

Three weeks after the fire you can walk into the great saloon on the south front and stand on the beautifully bleached oak floor. The two magnificent marble chimneypieces survive in pristine condition at either end. Carved and gilded doorcases are virtually intact – so are the plaster wall panels. Humphry Repton's white and gold en suite bookcases are largely undamaged. Only the rich coved ceiling has completely gone.

Martin Drury, the Trust's historic buildings secretary, points out how Nathaniel Dance's great portraits of George III and Queen Charlotte can go straight back to their original gilt plaster frames over the chimneypieces... Sir Harry Fetherstonhaugh over the central door and the Batonis, Zuccarellis and Giordanos around the rest of the walls.

The saving of the contents of the main rooms speaks wonders for the National Trust's staff and volunteers – and the cool professionalism of the firemen. ....'

He was positive about the future:

A really careful reconstruction such as the Trust will undertake at Uppark sets new standards for understanding every aspect of a building's construction, fitting out, decoration and furnishing. Like it or not, historic buildings are being repaired and done up all the time. What we need are the highest standards of craftsmanship. Uppark gives the Trust the opportunity – and the challenge – to show the very best that can be done.

Faced with disaster, we must not simply give up. The beauty of the past will survive only if we show equal determination that it shall not disappear before the ravages of all kinds – of the elements, of decay, of pressure from development.

None the less, the National Trust had set itself an enormous task. In the end its decision would be judged by the results. Would its faith in repair be rewarded? Would it really be possible to reassemble and incorporate all

the salvaged fragments? Whereas a large pool of skilled craftsmen and conservators could be drawn upon, few had ever worked together on a project of such size. Over 250 craftsmen would be needed. Like all creative people, they did not necessarily consider that repair required as much or more skill as new work. Moreover, many of the techniques, for example free-hand modelling in lime plaster, had been in abeyance in Britain for a century and a half and needed to be rediscovered. Even if the house could be authentically restored, were the purists right? Would Uppark end up as a lifeless facsimile, or worse, a misguided fake or reproduction antique? The answer to these questions lay five years ahead, and the Trust, despite its misgivings, was determined to make the attempt.

The Saloon: (*left*) a photograph of the west wall and fireplace taken in 1910; (*right*) the fireplace wall after the fire showing that although the ceiling had collapsed, the marble chimneypiece was intact and the wall decoration was virtually complete. The paintings were salvaged.

3: Design and Reconstruction

THE ARCHITECTURAL HISTORY of Uppark begins in about 1690 when an Elizabethan house was rebuilt on an earlier site by Ford Grey, later 1st Earl of Tankerville, an unscrupulous but successful politician whose father had married the heiress to the estate. The house, described as 'new built' in 1695, is a good example of a particularly English domestic style that had evolved in the mid-seventeenth century and which had its origins

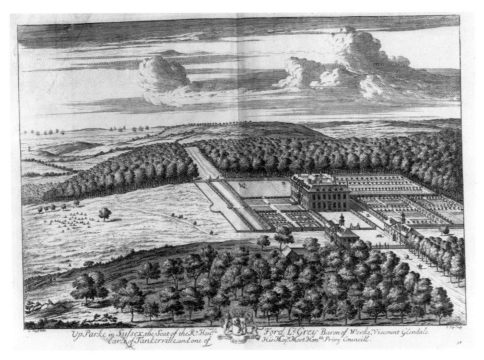

Left: Knyff and Kip's engraving of Uppark from the south-east published in their *Britannia Illustrata*, 1707.

Opposite: Fred Aldsworth, The Conservation Practice's archaeologist. He was responsible for gleaning precise measurements of every element of the building so that computer-aided drawings could be prepared.

in Inigo Jones's Serlio-inspired designs for astylar (plain-fronted) buildings such as those flanking St Paul's Church, in Covent Garden, or the house built for Lord Maltravers at Lothbury, in the City of London. In the 1660s it was perfected by Sir Roger Pratt (1620–84) at Clarendon House, in Piccadilly, and at Coleshill, in Berkshire (both now destroyed). Its hall-marks are simple, symmetrical and well-proportioned elevations and a

BEDROOM
BED-SITTING ROOM
YELLOW BEDROOM BATHROOM
DINING ROOM
RED DRAWING ROOM
STONE HALL
EXHIBITION ROOM
SOUTH PASSAGE
EAST CELLAR
THE CONSERVATION PRACT
SCALE 1:50
DATE APR.1990
DRAWN P F W
Dwg no UPPA 2010:60
JOB UPPARK
TITLE CROSS SECTION B-B LOOKING NORT
1 0 1 2 3 4 5m

A cross sectional elevation by The Conservation Practice showing the house looking north.

steep hipped roof carried on a projecting cornice. Distinction is imparted to the principal façade by projecting the three central bays and crowning them with a pediment, which, in the case of Uppark, contained a carved armorial cartouche. It is a sophisticated architectural tradition, deriving its proportions from the classical orders without overtly displaying them.

The architect employed by the future Lord Tankerville to design his new house is not known, but in 1815 James Dallaway, the historian of West Sussex, attributed Uppark to William Talman (1650–1719), Comptroller of the King's Works to William III. Although there is no evidence for Talman's employment at Uppark, the attribution is credible, and Talman would have been known to Tankerville, who was the King's First Commissioner of the Treasury and Lord Privy Seal.

The exterior and ground-floor plan of Uppark have remained little changed since Lord Tankerville's day. The house consists of two storeys

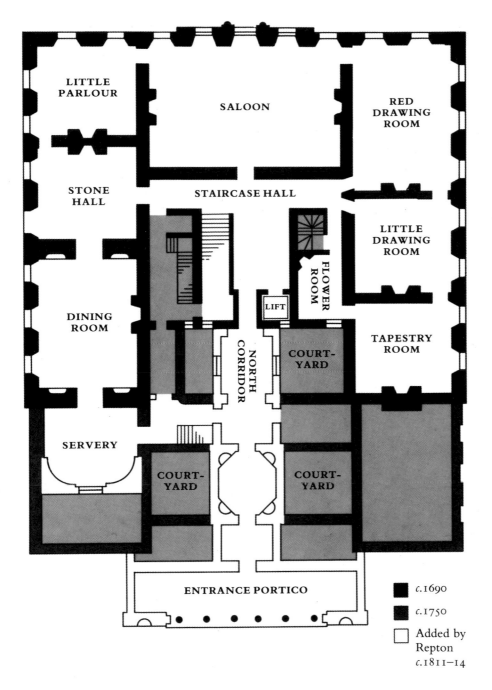

LITTLE
PARLOUR

SALOON

RED
DRAWING
ROOM

STONE
HALL

STAIRCASE HALL

LITTLE
DRAWING
ROOM

FLOWER
ROOM

LIFT

DINING
ROOM

NORTH
CORRIDOR

COURT-
YARD

TAPESTRY
ROOM

SERVERY

COURT-
YARD

COURT-
YARD

ENTRANCE PORTICO

■ c.1690

■ c.1750

□ Added by
Repton
c.1811–14

The ground-floor plan of Uppark

and an attic over a semi-basement. The main façade faces south and is nine bays wide, the centre three breaking forward and carrying the pediment. The east and west elevations are more or less identical; each has seven bays, the central one being treated as a pedimented doorway. The walls are of fine red brick; the quoins, string courses and window architraves are of white Portland stone. The north side, the back of the house, was treated in a simpler manner, with a recessed centre. The prominent hipped roof was originally covered in red clay tiles and had little square dormer windows, with alternating triangular and semicircular pediments, and tall, plain brick chimneystacks.

On the ground floor, two apartments, each with its parlour, bedchamber and closet, flanked a central axis comprising two large halls: the Marble Hall (now the Saloon) and the Staircase Hall. Originally, the Marble Hall was the main room of the house and rose through two storeys, with a pair of fireplaces flanking a large central door to the Staircase Hall. It may have taken its name from its marble pavement, just as the every-day entrance hall on the east front was called the Stone Hall after its flagged floor (which survives). Many of the rooms had bolection-moulded panelling, and the principal staircase, of oak, had a handsome barley-sugar twist balustrade.

In 1747 the 2nd Earl of Tankerville sold Uppark for £19,000 to the Northumbrian baronet Sir Matthew Fetherstonhaugh (1714–74), who had inherited a large fortune from a distant kinsman. He immediately set about a series of alterations and improvements at Uppark, briefly noted in his account book (destroyed in the fire). For instance, on 18 February 1747 he recorded £57 15s 6d paid 'On acct. of building at Uppark'. This phase of work also probably included the upgrading of the domestic offices, and by 1749 he had spent no less than £7,500 on building works and on the acquisition of furniture and furnishings. Two low projecting wings at basement and ground level were added to the north front, incorporating a new servants' hall and kitchen. Sir Matthew also replaced the Tankerville arms in the pediment of the south front with his own device. (The displaced Tankerville achievement can still be seen built into the front of an old farm house in the nearby village of Rake.)

Between 1749 and 1751 Sir Matthew was away on a Grand Tour of Italy where he acquired numerous pictures and some outstanding furniture. On his return he embarked, concurrently, on the erection of a fine London house, in Whitehall, to the design of James Paine (1717–89), and the embellishment of the suite of reception rooms along the west front of Uppark, as well as the Little Parlour and Stone Hall on the east side. The Staircase Hall was also altered; a Venetian window was inserted in the north wall, and the upper walls and ceilings were decorated with Neo-classical and rococo plasterwork. The two western drawing-rooms were given splendid rococo plaster ceilings and handsome carved marble chimneypieces *en suite*; the walls were hung with flock papers. It is uncertain whether Paine

Sir Matthew
Fetherstonhaugh, a
portrait painted in Rome
during his Grand Tour
by Pompeo Batoni in
1751, now hanging in
the Red Drawing Room
at Uppark (see p.136).

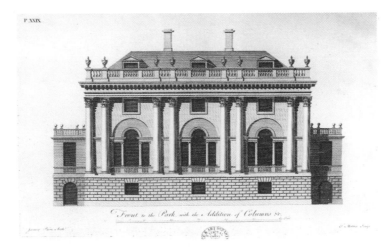

Sir Matthew's London
house in Whitehall,
showing the west front,
overlooking Green Park.
The house was built by
James Paine between
1754 and 1758 at a cost
of just over £10,000;
from Paine's 'Plans . . .
of Noblemen and
Gentlemen's Houses',
1767.

was responsible for the work at Uppark as well as in Whitehall, but since several craftsmen were employed in both houses, notably Thomas Carter for the chimneypieces, it seems a likelihood.

In about 1770 Sir Matthew began his final and most splendid phase of remodelling at Uppark, including the creation of the Saloon in place of Lord Tankerville's two-storeyed Marble Hall. The ceiling was lowered by inserting a mezzanine floor of bedrooms and dressing-rooms above, and the room was entirely redecorated in a fashionable Neo-classical manner which showed the influence of the Adam style. Again, although documentation is lacking, Paine was probably responsible for the architectural design. The Little Parlour in the south-east corner was also redecorated and given a Neo-classical ceiling with inset medallions.

Sir Matthew Fetherstonhaugh died in 1774 and was succeeded by his son Harry, who carried out further improvements to Uppark in the early nineteenth century with the assistance of his friend Humphry Repton, the landscape architect. In 1810, Repton outlined his plans for Uppark in his Red Book, and building work was carried out between 1812 and 1813. The principal alteration was to move the main entrance to the north side, where Repton erected a Tuscan portico between Sir Matthew's c.1750 office wings. Repton's alterations to the Dining Room included the insertion of mirrored alcoves, and bronzed panels and busts by George Garrard (1760–1827) into the north and south walls, as well as the provision of a Servery in part of the upper space of Sir Matthew's kitchen. Repton was also responsible for the white and gold decoration in both the Saloon and the Dining Room, which has survived every vicissitude including the 1989 fire.

When he was over seventy, Sir Harry married his twenty-year-old dairymaid, Mary Ann Bullock, to whom he bequeathed Uppark in 1846. Neither she nor her younger sister Frances, who joined the ménage as a child and outlived her sister, carried out any significant structural alterations. Some of the rooms were redecorated with French and English wallpapers, and in c.1865 the tiles on the outer roof slopes were replaced with slates; taller, segmental-topped dormers were inserted at the same time. After the dairymaid's death in 1874 hardly anything was changed. At the time of the fire in 1989, Uppark remained largely as it had been in the nineteenth century, even preserving its old paint, gilding and wallpapers.

In November 1989, after several architects had been interviewed, The Conservation Practice, a local Sussex firm based in Midhurst, was appointed to oversee the restoration of Uppark. It had been founded by Daryl Fowler, formerly of the Greater London Council's Historic Buildings Division (where he had been the architect responsible for the restoration of Covent Garden Market). The Conservation Practice specialised in repair and restoration and had its own in-house archaeologists and historians as well as designers who were supplemented by new recruits as the project progressed.

Sir Harry Fetherston-haugh, a portrait painted in Rome during his Grand Tour by Pompeo Batoni in 1776, now hanging in the Red Drawing Room. Sir Harry's portrait is on a grander scale than his father's (p.55) and would have been much more expensive due to the rise in Batoni's fame over the ensuing twenty-five years.

Uppark from the south-east by Humphry Repton, from his Red Book of 1810. His recommended alterations, executed between 1811 and 1815, were largely confined to the house: the arcades linking the house and flanking pavilions, proposed in this water-colour, were never built.

The architect in charge was Iain McLaren, who had been involved in the conservation of old buildings since the mid-1970s, when he had surveyed the historic Royal Dock Yard, at Chatham, and supervised the re-construction of the interiors of Richmond Terrace, in Whitehall, for the government. Paul Drury, the in-house adviser on the construction of eigh-teenth-century plaster, played a significant part in the early stages. Jeremy Poll, one of the assistant architects, was closely involved in supervising the joinery and plasterwork in the second half of the contract.

The architects' first task was to reinforce the scaffolding and to build a temporary roof to protect the interior from the weather until the house itself could be made permanently watertight. This in itself was an ambitious undertaking. Twenty miles of scaffold poles on 17,000 fixings were used. Two months into the contract, however, disaster struck. During the severe storms over southern England at the beginning of 1990 the temporary roof blew off, tragically killing two workmen. The site had been cleared because of the fierce south-westerly winds blowing up on 25 January, but

In the storms of 25 January 1990, the newly completed scaffolding and temporary roof were destroyed, causing the tragic deaths of two workmen. The roof, rebuilt with difficulty, was not completed until that August.

the two men had returned to collect their tools. As they did so, sections of the corrugated-iron roof were torn away and crushed them. With the temporary roof gone – and immensely difficult to replace – Uppark was left open to the weather for several months during the worst time of year, and the interior suffered further damage. This tragic set-back was the lowest point in the whole project, and greatly depressed the spirits of all those engaged in the enterprise.

Apart from the ill-fated temporary roof, other preliminary site works were completed in the autumn of 1989 and early 1990. All the debris was cleared, a new vehicular access was constructed and a village of sheds, stores and workshops was erected on the west lawn. The latter included the so-called Miracle Span Shed, a large covered space of 4,596 square yards

(350m), which proved extremely useful for a number of purposes, including the full-scale setting-out of the plasterwork for the ceilings. After the completion of building work, it was moved to the car-park in 1995 to house an exhibition on the fire and restoration of the house.

The design team, led by the architects, included Baker Wilkins Smith (Quantity Surveyors), Hockley & Dawson (Structural Engineering Consultants), and Gifford & Partners (Building Services Consultants). John Lelliott Ltd of New Malden, in Surrey, was appointed as the Management Contractor, with Ray Carter as Site Manager. In the 1980s Lelliott had been one of the largest and most successful building contractors in London, and had been involved in the repair of the Palace of Westminster, the Tower of London and Lambeth Palace. Badly hit by the recession, the firm went into liquidation and was taken over by Bovis half-way through the Uppark contract. As Ray Carter was taken on by Bovis Lelliott, however, there was continuity of site management throughout the contract.

In the early stages the Sun Alliance loss adjusters attended the design panel meetings and were given copies of all the architectural paperwork. As it was paying for the work, the insurance company had a fundamental interest in the design and construction programme. One of its requirements was that the work should proceed rapidly without delays so as to reduce the costs. The National Trust negotiated a rationale with the loss adjusters whereby the ground-floor rooms would be painstakingly repaired using traditional, and expensive, methods and materials – including lime and hair plaster on riven chestnut laths – but that more modern, and economical, materials could be used on the upper residential floors, with the plastering there being executed on an expanded metal mesh base, but still using lime plaster.

As the upper floors were to be totally rebuilt internally, the work had to comply with current Building Regulations, including means of escape. It proved relatively easy to render the upper floors fire-resistant with the use of 'Supalux', a proprietary fire-resisting board, with mineral wool quilt between the joists. It was not possible to provide a protected means of escape at ground-floor level (through the state-rooms), but a waiver was obtained for two new routes leading to the basement with fire-exit doors under the steps on the east and west sides of the house. In contrast to the repair work, minor alterations of this type required Listed Building Consent in the usual way from Chichester District Council and English Heritage. All this statutory procedure was dealt with in the first half of 1990, while a second temporary roof was being constructed.

The contract proper started on 18 June 1990 and was planned to run for four years. This timetable was maintained. Initially, the contract was intended to be divided into two parts, the first consisting of the reroofing, the repair of the fabric and the creation of a weathertight shell, and the second of the reinstatement of the interior. If Lelliott gave satisfaction in

View north-west, showing
the rebuilding of the
roof: May 1991 (*right*);
and November 1991
(*opposite*).

the first phase it was to be invited to manage the subsequent and more
extensive contract as well. In the event, there was no break and, as it turned
out, any interruption would have been impractical as the two stages over-
lapped with, for example, the structural work still proceeding in the Staircase Hall while the other ground-floor rooms had moved on to the joinery
and plaster contracts.

Fortnightly design team meetings, chaired by Iain McLaren, were held
throughout the contract. They were attended by the three groups directly
involved in the work: the National Trust, the professional consultants
and the management contractor. The Trust's representatives included the
Managing Agent at Uppark, Peter Pearce, assisted by Kevin Whitehead, a
quantity surveyor; Christopher Rowell; Nigel Seeley, the Trust's Surveyor
of Conservation, who played an important role in drawing up many of the
technical briefs; and on occasions Julian Prideaux, the Chief Agent and
chairman of the internal Uppark Steering Group, whose purpose was to set
the overall policy for the restoration.

An advisory panel, composed of independent members of the Trust's
various committees, also provided expert advice under the chairmanship
of Mrs Selina Ballance (chairman of the architectural panel). For the fortnightly meetings at Uppark the architects prepared discussion papers

which formed the basis for technical briefs and specifications. The outline schedule of work, with the principal procurement dates, was settled at the beginning. Thereafter the work was let in individual trade packages, organised by Lelliott, to the various works contractors, roofers, bricklayers and so forth, who executed their individual jobs in sequence. The advantages of this method of proceeding were many: the repair of the shell of the building could start immediately, rather than wait until all the design work had been completed, as is the case with an ordinary 'lump sum' building contract; the cost of the work could be carefully monitored, package by package, and necessary adjustments made as it progressed; and, perhaps most importantly, the design team had a direct influence on the selection of firms invited to tender for each package, thereby ensuring that only those with the requisite experience and skills could take part.

The first stage of the contract involved the repair of the outer shell. This included the partial rebuilding of the upper part of the north side of the house and the replacement of the Venetian window lighting the Staircase Hall. When this was completed in May 1991, the temporary metal roof and extra scaffold supports were removed to enable the carpenters and slaters to finish the roof proper. The shell was weathertight by June and the chimneys, pediment and windows were all finished by August. This first phase of building work cost £4.5 million and an idea of its scale can be gained from the statistics: 350 tonnes of oak were used in the roof structure and 45 tonnes of lead went to line the gutters, to form the ridges and to make the new flashings round the dormers and chimneys. The agreed aim was to use traditional materials and methods as far as was reasonably possible. Thus, lime mortar was employed for all the work, and the new roof was made, as before, of oak and Baltic deals, and was not steel-framed.

This approach was dictated by conservation and aesthetic requirements. The use of traditional materials and methods in the course of repairing and reconstructing the fabric of the house has retained an overall structural consistency which should enhance its long-term survival. At the same time, the characteristic movement and ageing process of timber and lime mortar will undoubtedly, over time, give back to the place many of those subtle qualities that distinguished Uppark before the fire, especially the slight unevenness of line and texture which provide so much of the visual charm of an old building. Thus, the roof slates will gradually ripple as their wooden supports settle, and the salvaged fragments of original plaster will remain in harmony with replacement lime plasterwork.

In selecting subcontractors and craftsmen, the National Trust asked for samples of work, to be approved by the design team, as a preliminary to tenders, so that it could be sure that the work would be of the required quality and that only fully competent firms would compete for the job. The slating and tiling contract was awarded to the London Welsh Roofing Company Ltd, of Oxted, in Surrey. This family-owned company, known for its traditional high-quality roofing work, is active throughout south-east England. Other recent contracts have included work at Chiddingstone Castle, in Kent, and the Old Bailey and Buckingham Palace, in London.

The new roof is illustrative of the pragmatic decisions that were made as the work progressed. When the house was first rebuilt in the seventeenth century, it was almost certainly roofed with red tiles. These survived on the inner slopes at the time of the fire, but the outer faces had been renewed at different dates, partly with green Welsh slates, and partly with Cornish Delabole slates. It was decided to clad all the outer slopes of the roof in Delabole slates because they are still available (the green-slate quarry had closed and would have been prohibitively expensive to reopen). However, as Delabole slates are no longer produced in the larger sizes, the grading of the slates could not match the roof's pre-fire appearance. The inner slopes were covered with red tiles, as before.

Beneath the roof, the timber cornice, with 132 modillions (projecting brackets), was entirely rebuilt. A few of the modillions were salvaged and reinstated after repair but most had to be recarved, using laminated oak, by Bakers of Danbury. The chimneys also had to be largely rebuilt and 43 new pots were made as exact copies of the few surviving originals. The replacements, which varied in size and design, were hand-thrown by

Mick Pinner, a local potter from West Meon, in Hampshire. Reviving an old tradition of inscribing chimneypots, he engraved on one: 'Margaret Thatcher resigned as I was making this.' He chose a special clay designed to withstand the elements and provided the pots with lids to prevent birds falling down the disused chimneys.

As the original roof had been totally destroyed, its shape had to be reconstructed using photogrammetric drawings derived from low oblique aerial photographs taken in the 1960s. The timber structure had to be deduced from various sources, including a survey made shortly before the fire. Very few roof timbers had been discovered in the debris (only four out of 592 structural timbers recovered and identified were from the roof), although there was evidence that the original structure had incorporated reused timber. Some fragments of the principal rafters and collars *in situ* were identifiable in photographs taken after the fire while the shell was being made safe. One small piece of wall-plate survived in the north-east corner, making it possible to reconstruct the section through the eaves. The main attic floor beams were carried on the wall-plate and a pole-plate on to which the principal and common rafters were slotted in or 'birds-mouthed'. The very few fragments of roof beams identified in the salvage operation, together with comparative evidence, indicated that the roof comprised principal rafters, purlins in line and common rafters tenoned into the purlins and notched over the pole-plates. This was consistent with known seventeenth-century practice, thus establishing that the original roof structure had survived until the 1989 fire. The south front pediment, however, had been remodelled by Sir Matthew Fetherstonhaugh in the

Left: As the roof had been almost completely destroyed, the carved wooden brackets or modillions supporting the cornice had to be recarved. Fortunately several originals survived and, having been used as models, were reinstated.

Right: Mick Pinner of West Meon Pottery throwing a new chimney-pot to replace those destroyed or damaged in the fire. The new pots exactly copied the design of the old.

A section of retrieved oak roof timber spliced, or 'birdsmouthed', to new wood of equally massive proportions. Although few original remnants survived the fire, the new roof structure was a copy of the essentially seventeenth-century arrangement.

eighteenth century, and the slate covering and dormer windows dated from *c.*1865, when Sir Harry's widow repaired the house.

All the Victorian dormer windows had, of course, disappeared in the fire. By good fortune, however, it turned out that a joiner who had repaired them in the 1970s still had one dormer, beyond repair, in his workshop, and this provided a model to copy. The original dormers of Lord Tankerville's house were square in proportion, with alternating triangular and segmental pediments (as recorded in Pieter Tillemans's painting, of *c.*1725, hanging in the Staircase Hall, and in Knyff and Kip's 1707 engraved bird's-eye view). That no attempt was made to return to the original *c.*1690 dormer design, though it was well recorded, was one instance of the Trust's declared policy of restoring the house to 'the day before the fire' and not making any changes on aesthetic or historical grounds.

The new leadwork on the roof was not welded. There was to be no opportunity for a repeat of the previous disaster. After the fire, the Trust had issued instructions that no 'hot-work' should be done on its premises. This blanket prohibition goes much further than the requirements of any other institution, including English Heritage. The prohibition on hot-work was upheld, partly by using only machine-cast Code 7 or 8 lead, which was 'bossed' in the traditional manner by beating it into shape with wooden

mallets, rather than by welding. Unavoidable hot-work, such as making the welded rainwater exits from the gutters, was undertaken in a detached shed with a strict fire-watching regime. The rainwater pipes were also prepared in this hut.

All the lead downpipes and gutters were custom-built, as before the fire, but there was one practical improvement. The cornice gutter along the south front at Uppark had always caused problems. A history of dry rot in the Saloon below was the result of rainwater overflowing and soaking the front wall. The gutter was too shallow and did not have enough steps in it to carry the rain away. The architects wished to cure this defect by inserting two lead downpipes in the re-entrant angles of the projecting pedimented central bay. English Heritage's inspector at first opposed this as a material alteration to the appearance of the building. It proved possible, however, to make a convincing case on the precedent of other buildings of the period and also by drawing English Heritage's attention to the way in which the stone string course stopped short of the corners of the break-front, indicating that downpipes in this position had originally been intended. Listed Building Consent was therefore forthcoming.

The background stonework of the pediment supporting the carved achievement of the Fetherstonhaugh arms had crumbled in the heat.

Pieter Tillemans's painting of Uppark from the south-east, probably painted in the 1720s for the Staircase Hall. It provides an invaluable record of the appearance of the house as it was built, *c.*1690, with the stables and laundry blocks to the east of the main house. The central pediment of the house carries the original Tankerville arms.

[65]

The Fetherstonhaugh coat-of-arms within the pediment survived the fire virtually intact, but its stone support had to be replaced.

The stonework was renewed by Cathedral Works Organisation Ltd, of Chichester, the firm which executed the masonry contract, while Trevor Proudfoot of the Cliveden Conservation Workshop, in Buckinghamshire, repaired and refixed the heraldry, replacing part of the carving in the process. All the external stonework was completed by May 1992, when the last of the scaffolding was removed.

From the outside, Uppark looked its old self once more. As if to mark this, and to give the reroofed house nature's seal of approval, the house martins returned that spring to nest in the cornice, as they had done before the fire. There was something almost uncanny about the repaired exterior. It seemed impossible that a building which had undergone such a trauma could look so serene and timeless with its beautifully weathered brick façades entirely unmarked by scorching or smoke. It was a great mercy that the Staircase Hall had acted like a giant chimney and drawn all the smoke and flames inwards and upwards, thereby preventing any external fire damage around the windows. The only scars had been extensive blotches of molten lead from the roof, which had splashed off the scaffold boards on to the brickwork but these had proved comparatively easy to remove. The windows sparkled once more in the sunlight, thanks to their uneven panes. The surviving glass in the old sashes consisted of various types. The new glass, the nearest equivalent to nineteenth-century crown glass with a similar uneven texture, was cylinder glass known as *verre royale*. This was manufactured in France, there being no equivalent made in Britain.

The repair of the external walls included rebuilding a displaced section at the top corner of the south front, for which enough salvaged bricks were available, as well as a larger section of the upper part of the north front, where new, matching, hand-made bricks were used. The structural work inside the house continued after the external shell was completed. This involved patching and stitching the internal walls, as well as rebuilding the floors using the salvaged timbers supplemented by new boards of seasoned oak. Some of the beams were spliced, cutting out charred sections and inserting new pieces. Interesting details, such as the reuse of seventeenth-century sash frames as joists in the Red Drawing Room floor, were conscientiously retained. Evidence for the reconstruction of the destroyed upper floors was derived from the pockets in the masonry for the beams and joists and fragments of the latter excavated in the post-fire salvage. The lintels over the doors were renewed in concrete, not timber, because of the danger of dry rot and settlement. These lintels were among a number of new introductions inserted only where they are invisible. Some of the first-floor rooms have been insulated with modern wall-linings to keep in the heat, and the whole house is protected with fireproof boarding behind the new lath and plaster surfaces to create a series of controllable zones, divided by fire-resisting doors and walls.

The domestic services are also all new, but remarkably unobtrusive and are hardly noticed by most visitors to the house. The heating, designed to maintain the relative humidity at an appropriate conservation level, is set beneath metal grilles (copied from one in the basement) in the floors of the window embrasures in the principal rooms to replace the defunct 1930s radiators. The electric lighting is provided either from the old chandeliers, lanterns and sconces (which had been wired for electricity in the 1930s) or from old table lamps with skirting sockets. To these have been added some newly purchased antique colza oil lights and candle lustres converted to electricity to achieve an acceptable level of lighting for public viewing. The new heating, lighting, fire and security arrangements all draw on the latest technology. No attempt has been made to repeat the former arrangements; on the contrary, the opportunity has been taken to update them. The new pipes and wire conduits running through the basement are a visible modern adjunct, representing the Trust's general policy to upgrade the technology while restoring the building fabric and decoration exactly to its pre-fire date. Even here, however, a precedent was followed, as visible pipework was first introduced into the basement in the nineteenth century.

The accuracy of the architects' drawings for the interior depended upon the post-fire surveys, both archaeological and photogrammetric, as well as

Structural timbers retrieved from the house, laid out on the lawn soon after the fire.

The Red Drawing Room floor before the floor-boards were laid, showing seventeenth-century window frames recycled as floor joists in the mid-eighteenth century.

the National Trust's archive of photographs. Under the direction of Fred Aldsworth, The Conservation Practice's archaeologist, all this material was used to produce detailed drawings which were computer-plotted to scale. A computerised 'library' was built up of all the architectural details – skirtings, mouldings, architraves and so forth – to assist the draughtsmen. Thus, by using the most modern methods available, the contractors were guided by accurate drawings, and this made it easier to achieve an almost exact restoration and reconstruction of the building.

Much came to light about the original form of Lord Tankerville's house and the subsequent alterations by Sir Matthew and Sir Harry Fetherston-haugh. At the request of the Trust, Fred Aldsworth prepared illustrated reports on the archaeological discoveries for archive purposes as well as to assist with the restoration. Of particular interest was the new evidence for the internal layout of the original house. This made it possible to re-consider and corroborate the 1705 inventory of Uppark prepared four years after the death of the 1st Earl of Tankerville. The internal masonry structure was widely exposed, revealing the original positions of doors, windows, fireplaces and room partitions. The chief discovery was that the Saloon, the 'Greate Hall' of the 1705 inventory, originally rose through two storeys and had a pair of chimneypieces on the north wall (where Repton's bookcases now are) flanking a very large central door to the Staircase Hall. It used to be thought that Sir Matthew had created the Saloon in c.1770 by raising the pre-existing ceiling; in fact, he lowered the room by inserting the mezzanine above, incorporating the Print Room and two flanking rooms. The lines of the original dado, and the cornice at second-floor level, could be discerned in the newly exposed brickwork.

In the Stone Hall, it was discovered that the fireplace was originally in the centre of the north wall and was moved to its present position when the central door was made to the Dining Room in the mid-eighteenth century. It also turned out that the stone floor did not date from the construction of the house but was a slightly later insertion. Some of the slabs are of recycled Jacobean masonry, one of them having carved decoration with a lion's head, ribbons and leaves on its reverse. Much medieval stonework had also been reused in the structure of the house.

The post-fire investigations also helped to clarify the problem of the Dining Room and proved that it was not a surviving seventeenth-century room, as used to be thought. It was originally two rooms, each with a central fireplace (where the doors now are). Evidence for the dividing partition, a third of the way up the existing room, was discovered in the floor structure and in a break in the plaster on the west wall, beneath the panelling. This was corroborated by the 1705 inventory which referred to 'My Lords Bedchamber' and 'The Parlor Next'. The north and south walls, with their central doorways, mirrored alcoves and plaster plaques, were alterations by

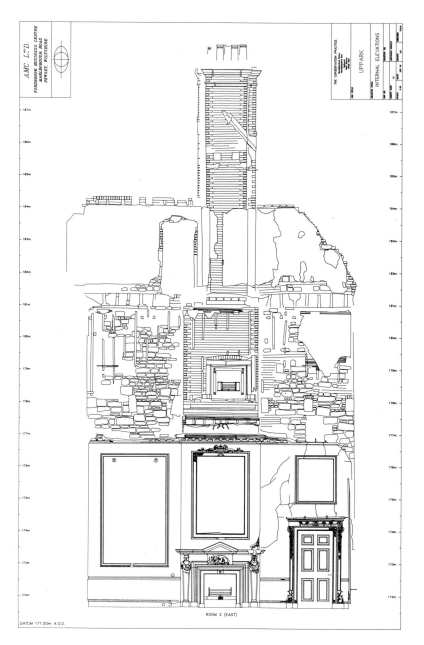

A computer-aided drawing produced by The Conservation Practice of the east wall of the Saloon, and the severely damaged bedroom above.

Repton between 1812 and 1814, as is indicated by their differing materials, including some deal joinery.

Throughout the house, fireplaces and doorways had been moved around or modified. The Staircase Hall originally had a central fireplace in the north wall (in place of the present doorway from Repton's corridor) and the Venetian window above had been inserted through its flue in *c.*1750, replacing a pair of flanking sash-windows. Some of the first-floor bedrooms had started off with corner fireplaces, which had been removed in the mid-eighteenth century. On the ground floor, all the doors connecting the principal rooms had been narrowed and moved slightly away from the outer wall, to create a better *enfilade* as part of Sir Matthew's alterations in the mid-eighteenth century.

The main rooms on the ground and first floors had originally been lined with bolection-moulded panelling and several were hung with tapestries, woven textiles or gilt leather (surviving nail holes indicate their outline). When Sir Matthew had modernised and redecorated most of these rooms, he had kept, or reused, some of the framework of the *c.*1690 wall-panelling made up with old window soffits and other bits and pieces to form timber linings under the new wall-coverings; he had even recycled some of the seventeenth-century window frames as floor joists. These have all been retained, where they survived the fire, as part of the history of the house. Detailed drawings and photographs constitute a record of what is new in the restored ground floor and basement. While, generally speaking, these rooms were substantially intact, much less evidence existed for the upper floors. There were far fewer photographs and surviving fragments of the first-floor bedrooms, which until the fire retained a considerable proportion of their seventeenth-century bolection-moulded panelling as well as beautifully carved mid-eighteenth-century chimneypieces and old wallpapers. The central room on the mezzanine floor, over the Saloon, was the charming eighteenth-century Print Room with engravings pasted to the original background paper. Mercifully, these engravings and their backing had been removed for conservation before the fire and so escaped the flames. This is now the only room at this level which preserves its original décor. The other first-floor rooms had to be reconstructed to their previous appearance on the evidence of archive photographs. Only the Georgian and Victorian fireplaces survived, and these have been restored. The wooden fire surrounds have been recarved by Alan Lamb and Paddy Little, and the panelling remade by Ashby & Horner, the main joinery contractors for the whole house. Apart from the Print Room, which has been opened on a monthly basis, the first floor and part of the second floor are now once again the private home of the Meade-Fetherstonhaugh family.

4: The Plasterwork

THE KEY ELEMENT in the restoration of Uppark's interiors was the ceiling plasterwork, all of which had collapsed. If it could be successfully recreated, then everything else, it was hoped, would fall into place. The problem was that the art of *in situ* free-hand modelling of lime and hair plaster had been lost for about 150 years. No plastering firm in Britain had any experience of such work and no other British post-war restorations of seventeenth- and eighteenth-century plaster decoration had been executed in an authentic manner. Schemes such as the reconstruction of the Wren churches in the City of London or the Assembly Rooms in Bath, for instance, had employed cast gypsum and fibrous plaster, a much easier technique, but anachronistic and comparatively mechanical and lifeless. Not only did the Uppark stucco require the revival of forgotten skills, but the scale of work was daunting. No fewer than five decorative ceilings, all of extremely elaborate design, needed to be completely rebuilt. To make the task even more difficult, hundreds of fragments of the ceiling enrichments salvaged from the wreckage after the fire were to be incorporated in the new plasterwork.

It was not clear that it could be done, but in the event the challenge was met. The country was scoured for suitable artists and craftsmen with the capacity to master the lost techniques. In the view of the Trust's Managing Agent at Uppark, Peter Pearce, the achievement of the Uppark plasterwork team was the 'greatest glory' of the restoration of the house. So successful was the final result that it is impossible to tell which parts of the ceilings were modelled in the mid-eighteenth century and which in the 1990s. Part of the secret of this success has been the collaboration between good professional plasterers and artists, who brought differing experience to bear on what could well have been an intractable problem.

The decorative plasterwork at Uppark was executed for Sir Matthew Fetherstonhaugh, and his wife Sarah, in the mid-eighteenth century. Stylistically, the ceilings fall into two groups, reflecting the two phases of Sir Matthew's interior reconstructions in *c.*1750 and *c.*1770. The Staircase Hall, the Red Drawing Room and the Little Drawing Room ceilings were all executed in the rococo style, whereas the Saloon and the Little Parlour date from the second phase and show the influence of the 'Adam revolution'.

Anne King, one of the plasterers from the Cliveden Conservation Workshop, putting the finishing touches to a section of the Red Drawing Room ceiling.

[73]

The Red Drawing Room: (*right*) photographed in 1956. The plasterwork ceiling, installed *c.*1750 and originally plain white, was decorated in blue and white in the early nineteenth century; (*below*) in 1994, after restoration. The ceiling incorporating original salvaged elements, repeated the nineteenth-century colour scheme.

Before Sir Matthew and his wife left England in 1749 for their two-year Grand Tour of the principal Italian cities, they had already begun the initial phase of a substantial rebuilding and redecoration programme. This was to continue until 1756 at least, with some bills not being settled until 1759. These suggest that the main building works were undertaken in the period from 1747 to 1759; a letter written by Sir Matthew in September 1766, however, implies that some work was still in hand, and his last phase of alterations began in 1770.

It is not always clear from Sir Matthew's accounts whether the payments listed relate to Uppark or to his new town house, as he was working on both properties simultaneously. The London house, occupying a splendid position overlooking Horse Guards' Parade, in Whitehall, was built between 1754 and 1758. (Later known as Dover House, it is now the Scottish Office.) It is possible that its architect, James Paine, was also responsible for

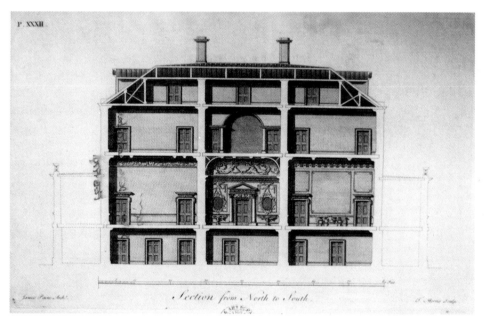

Cross-section of Sir Matthew Fetherston-haugh's house in Whitehall showing the original decorative scheme designed by James Paine in the 1750s. The plasterwork and furniture are similar to contemporary work at Uppark; from Paine's 'Plans . . . of Noblemen and Gentlemen's Houses', 1767.

the designs of the remodelled interiors at Uppark, but there is no proof. Certainly the plasterwork echoes the two stages in the development of Paine's style of interior decoration, which moved from the rococo forms of the western range of rooms towards the Neo-classical manner, employing compartmented ceilings and scrolled festoons in an attempt to rival the fashionable new style of the Adam brothers, in the Saloon and Little Parlour.

Paine's plasterer at Whitehall was Joseph Rose the Elder (1723–80), who became the leading English plasterer of his day. He employed a large atelier, and his plasterwork stands out for its unfailing technical perfection. His son Joseph Rose the Younger (1745–99) took on his father's mantle and worked extensively for Robert Adam and James and Samuel Wyatt. The elder Rose's work for Sir Matthew Fetherstonhaugh marked a turning point in his career. Sir Matthew himself recorded that Rose had been recommended to him by Paine, and that his plastering for the White-hall house (for which he was paid 'in full' in May 1758) was Rose's first work in the capital. Rose had wished to live in London, and through his commission from Sir Matthew 'got into some of the best Businesses' there. Rose's London connection with Sir Matthew and with Paine argues for his involvement at Uppark, but there is no documentary evidence. None the less, Rose was paid by Sir Matthew's executors in 1774 for plasterwork in a banqueting house, the so-called Vandalian Tower, at Uppark, and the 1750s rococo plasterwork elsewhere is closely comparable to Rose's contemporary work at Felbrigg, in Norfolk, also under Paine's direction.

Whereas Victorian and modern plasterwork is made of gypsum, mid-eighteenth-century and earlier plasterwork, such as that of the Uppark ceilings, was based on lime and is chemically distinct. Only some decorative elements at Uppark, such as the four pre-cast oval reliefs in the ceiling of the Little Parlour and some of the ornaments in the Saloon ceiling, were made of cast gypsum plaster. The majority of the decorative plasterwork was lime-based. In simple chemistry, lime plaster is a product of calcium carbonate (chalk, limestone or marble), which is burnt to produce calcium oxide (quicklime) and when it is soaked in water produces calcium hydroxide. This sets by returning to carbonate through the absorption of carbon dioxide from the atmosphere, as the water produced in the reaction evaporates. For gypsum plasters, calcium sulphate (alabaster or gypsum) is heated to drive off most of the water, and it sets by rehydration. Lime plasters are relatively slow-setting, and easily worked in a plastic state. Linear mouldings, such as cornices, are usually run *in situ* using a template or 'horse' and decorative elements can either be worked up by hand using modelling tools or, in suitable cases, moulded. This may be done on the bench, with the fairly stiff plaster (stucco) being forced into a mould and then fixed in place; alternatively, in the case of continuous enrichment, it can be done *in situ* by hand or with a die. By contrast, gypsum plaster, being quick-setting, is not suited to hand-modelling *in situ*.

Eighteenth-century hand-modelling techniques produced plasterwork that was bold, lively and fluid, as, for example, in the foliage panels of the Red Drawing Room. The linear mouldings of the cornice and panel ribs were run *in situ* in lime plaster (incorporating sand and hair), with a fine white setting coat on the finished faces. The enrichments were executed in stucco forced into moulds in standard lengths. These were then fixed into place with a thin adhesive layer of plaster. Where a greater sharpness or depth was required, the moulded elements were enhanced with a spatula or knife, or the stucco was applied and modelled *in situ* using a metal (probably lead) die, whose impressions are evident on the plaster of the basic moulding in some cases. The foliage ornament was set out using scored lines on the finishing coat of plaster; it was then built up by hand, the heavier sections in two coats around iron nails or armatures. Some elements were moulded and then manipulated to blend in with the hand-modelled work. This build-up of ornament by overlaying elements such as leaves, flowers and fruit produced a great sense of depth and vitality.

The problem facing the Trust and the architects at Uppark was to assemble a team with the necessary technical ability and artistic flair to recapture these qualities, so different from those of routine modern cast and moulded gypsum or fibrous plasterwork. Relearning the techniques for executing the stucco work was only half the problem. The original mix for the plaster also had to be rediscovered. Samples of the original ceilings were analysed and the ingredients worked out. The original plasters ranged from a lime, sand and hair mix for the flat beds to pure lime putty for the moulded ornaments. Some of the plaster contained wood ash, which was probably an accidental contaminant resulting from the fuel used in the kiln.

After initial assessment by the Cliveden Conservation Workshop, further plaster analysis was carried out by Dr Graham Morgan of the Department of Archaeology at Leicester University. Dr Morgan is the leading English expert on early mortars and plasters and his researches were useful in preparing the specification for the authentic plaster mixes. The constituents of the plaster varied according to its situation. For instance, a hair lime plaster paste was used for the ceiling flats or beds, while that for the moulded plaster was a thicker mix, more like dough. A thinner slurry of gypsum plaster was used for the cast work. Most of the ceiling bed plaster

George Jackson & Sons, founded in 1780, cast the repetitive cornice and ceiling mouldings. Here, one of the plasterers prepares egg and dart mouldings.

was a 3:1 mix of sand and lime, with hair. This flatwork was built up in three coats. A thick coat was laid immediately on to the split chestnut laths and then two finer coats were added to give a smooth finish before the raised decorative plasterwork was applied. Most of the linear mouldings were new copies, but as much as possible of the salvaged free-hand decoration was incorporated alongside the new moulded work.

A crucial role in the recreation of the plaster was played by the Cliveden Conservation Workshop. This workshop was set up by the National Trust under the direction of Trevor Proudfoot, who had trained as a stone-mason, to advise on the repair and maintenance of the Trust's large accu-mulation of sculpture and sculpted ornament distributed between 200 properties. It is based in the old tennis court buildings on the Cliveden estate, in Buckinghamshire, earlier used as a hospital for Canadian troops during the First World War. Originally known as the National Trust Statuary Workshop, it became an independent company in 1990. While retaining its role with the National Trust, it now offers its services to a wide range of outside clients. In addition to its workshop at Cliveden, the company also has a carving shop in Bath, and has built up a team of craftsmen with a variety of expertise. The workshop's experience with free-hand carving proved in-valuable for the pioneering development of free-hand modelling in plaster.

A small panel comprising the architect, Nigel Seeley and Christopher Rowell from the Trust, Lelliott's Site Manager Ray Carter, Paul Drury of The Conservation Practice, and Trevor Proudfoot discussed the issues and assessed the type of craftsmen needed to tackle the job. They were looking for practical, imaginative people who could find their way through the problems presented – not necessarily for those with experience of plaster-work of the required type (only a few conservators had any acquaintance with this specialised field), but for enthusiasts with the requisite modelling skills who would learn as they went along.

There were three stages in the recreation of the ceilings. The first began while the house was still smouldering, when significant pieces of the original plasterwork were salvaged, including a complete cartouche with the Fether-stonhaugh crest from the ceiling of the Little Drawing Room. The plaster fragments were sorted by Fiona Allardyce, then the Trust's adviser on the conservation of wall-paintings, and by Richard Ireland and others from Cliveden. On the basis of their feasibility report, it did not take long to decide that the ceilings in the principal rooms should be recreated according to the original method and incorporating as many of the salvaged fragments as possible. It turned out to be feasible to include more of the original work than had been envisaged in the immediate post-fire discussions.

The second phase involved research into the original plaster composition, and the formation of a team to execute the work. The third stage was the contract proper. The panel had a reasonable idea of how eighteenth-century free-hand modelling was done. Before joining the architects' practice,

A section of the ceiling of the Little Drawing Room, dating from *c.*1750, incorporating the antelope crest of the Fetherstonhaughs. Retrieved soon after the fire and restored by Cliveden Conservation, it was reinstated in the ceiling. The oak laths supporting the plaster-work can be clearly seen.

Paul Drury had been employed by English Heritage (to which he has since returned) and had made a study of Joseph Rose's plasterwork at Audley End, in Essex, where evidence found beneath the floorboards had enabled him to reconstruct the working methods of Rose's travelling plaster work-shop; the results of his research were published in 1984. Trevor Proudfoot had recently been involved in a project which, with hindsight, might seem to have been a special preparation for the task at Uppark. This was the repair of Benjamin Carter's plaster reliefs of Olympian gods (dated 1764) in the Pantheon at Stourhead, in Wiltshire. Proudfoot had analysed their plaster mix and the techniques used in their manufacture. These proved to be identical to those evident in the Uppark ceilings, and enabled him to work out how free-hand modelling had been done in the eighteenth century.

A large number of plastering companies, both British and Continental, expressed interest in the Uppark project, and about ten were interviewed by the panel. Most had no experience of free-hand modelling and only four were deemed good enough to be considered for the next stage. They were asked to produce a full-scale sample of hand-modelled ceiling plaster-work, and were given the names of about twenty 'experts' in eighteenth-century plasterwork who might be able to help them. These ranged from the artist Christopher Hobbs, who had recreated free-hand in modern plaster the damaged and missing rococo plasterwork in the Menagerie at Horton, in Northamptonshire, for Gervase Jackson-Stops, to Deborah McCarthy of the Victoria & Albert Museum and the Cliveden Conservation Workshop itself. The two most competent examples were produced by Cliveden, as subcontractors to George Jackson & Sons, and St Blaise Ltd; both were asked to submit tenders. Both sample panels were encouraging. St Blaise's displayed competent flat work and good dentil and cornice details, whereas the Jacksons' panel had fair flat and cornice work, and good free-hand work, by Geoff Preston of Cliveden Conservation. Though somewhat awkward in appearance, his free-hand modelling showed obvious flair and understanding, partly no doubt because it was produced at Uppark by reference to the old fragments.

George Jackson & Sons – now part of Clark & Fenn, which, in turn, is owned by a larger conglomerate, Trafalgar House – has been one of the leading plaster firms in England for over 200 years. The company was founded in London in 1780 and has specialised in cast plasterwork, making its own composition ornament based on whiting, animal glues, oils and resin. Jacksons preserves a vast collection of over 20,000 carved boxwood moulds for plasterwork, dating from the eighteenth century. It has received a royal warrant from five sovereigns, and its many restoration projects have included work at Hampton Court and Brighton Pavilion. Its team of apprentice-trained master craftsmen, some of whom have forty years' experience, was well equipped for doing the beds of the ceilings, the cornices and all the cast mouldings and ornaments, although they had no knowledge of conservation, of working with traditional lime plaster or of free-hand modelling. To remedy these deficiencies Jacksons subcontracted the repair of surviving fragments and all the free-hand plaster enrichment of the ceilings to Trevor Proudfoot's Cliveden Conservation Workshop.

With the Uppark contract in mind, Trevor Proudfoot had already employed Geoff Preston, with whom he had trained as a stonemason. Through a friend, who had written a thesis on eighteenth-century stucco and had studied the ingredients and techniques employed, Geoff Preston had been introduced to William Millar's *Plastering, Plain and Decorative* (1897), which proved an invaluable work of reference. Preston not only masterminded the ceiling plasterwork, but also was closely involved in modelling the plaster wall decorations. His single-minded response to the task in hand pulled the team of modellers together, and his training as a stonemason ensured that the ceilings were properly set out before any plasterwork was worked *in situ.*

In assembling the ingredients for the plaster, the Cliveden Conservation Workshop was advised by the Geological Museum, in South Kensington. In the South Harting sand-pit they found a perfect silver sand, now much used for work of this type. Trevor Proudfoot was also able to secure some ten-year-old lime putty from the National Trust lime works at Hardwick, in Derbyshire. Thanks to the ubiquity of sand and Portland cement in run-of-the-mill English building work, where mortar and pointing is generally of a deplorably low standard, lime for plaster and mortar is now a rarity. Recently the National Trust has been active in reviving the use of lime for the repair of historic buildings and has established lime works in different regions to supply its own needs: at Hawkshead, in Cumbria, for the repair of Lakeland farmhouses and at Hardwick Hall, in Derbyshire, for the lengthy restoration programme at that great Elizabethan house. The older the lime putty, the more plastic and malleable it is. In the eighteenth century, plasterers used twelve-year-old lime for modelling plaster, but the ten-year-old product from Hardwick proved to be acceptable. The plaster for the ceiling beds was mixed with goat and cow hair to give it the necessary strength. This hair is now difficult to obtain and much of it had to be imported. The main ingredient of this mix was lime, with a little sand and hair.

Jacksons made all the egg and dart, guilloche and other lengths of repetitive mouldings, as well as all the new *paterae* and similar cast ornaments. There were no less than six sizes of *paterae* in the Saloon ceiling alone, each of which required a separate mould. To make moulded enrichments the 'green hard' lime putty was beaten into the moulds, then tipped out and finished by hand, the Cliveden craftsmen sometimes helping with these final touches. As a result, each of the ornaments was slightly different, giving the work a liveliness not found in standard moulded decoration. The cornices and mouldings were moulded in short sections and fixed in place with wet plaster. The architects were directly involved with the tradesmen in daily discussions on mixes and modelling details. The craftsmen considered the architects and the Trust to be hard taskmasters, who insisted on anything which they regarded as substandard being done again.

A plasterer working in Jackson's site workshops on the cast ribs of the Red Drawing Room ceiling.

There were some initial failures, but as work progressed, confidence grew and by the end it was as if everybody had been handling this medium all their lives.

Most of the free-hand plasterers were trained as artists. After Geoff Preston's sample had won, Cliveden had placed an advertisement in an artists' trade newsletter which elicited over twenty replies. Other names came forward by word-of-mouth recommendation. From this list eight were chosen; one was a painter of icons, some were art students, but most were sculptors. Each was required to produce a sample of a satisfactory standard before qualifying to work in the house. The eight were divided into two teams of four each, working simultaneously on the two ranges of rooms – the rococo Drawing Rooms and Staircase ceilings on the one hand, and the later Neo-classical Saloon and Little Parlour on the other – in order to meet the tight deadlines. As well as modelling all the free-hand decoration, Cliveden provided general advice on techniques and mixes throughout the plaster contract.

The process of reconstructing and copying the decorative ceilings began not in the house itself but in the Miracle Span Shed, the large pre-fabricated workshop on the east lawn. Here, large polythene sheets, the size of the ceilings, were laid out on the floor and the full-scale design of the plasterwork was traced on to them by The Conservation Practice's draughts-man using the 1:10 computer-aided scale drawings, derived from photo-graphs of the rooms taken before the fire, rectified by a series of measuring devices. Once the ceiling drawings had been laid out, the original plaster fragments salvaged from each room, and stored in bread-trays since their initial post-fire rescue and sorting, were placed where they belonged, like a giant jigsaw puzzle. The proportion of surviving old plaster varied from room to room depending on the ferocity of the fire – in the Staircase Hall only a small piece of foliage from the central rococo boss had been salvaged; by contrast, a large number of the mid-eighteenth-century enrichments from the Red Drawing Room were rescued and reused. When the Red Drawing Room ceiling was laid out on the scale drawing, many of the modillions presumed to have come from its cornice proved to be smaller ones which had fallen through from the ceiling of the room above. Altogether about 20 per cent of the original free-hand moulded plaster-work was reused in the restored ceilings.

Once delineated on the polythene sheets, the ceiling designs were accurately transferred and 'pounced' on to the plain bed of the relevant ceiling, prepared by Jacksons, ready for the plasterers to carry out their modelling *in situ*. 'Pouncing' was a technique employed by plasterers in the early eighteenth century, when numerous Italian-speaking Swiss stuc-cadores were working in Britain. They developed the plaster techniques which became general in the Georgian period, and which were revived for the Uppark restoration. The word derives from pumice (lava), a fine powder originally used in tracing patterns through pinprick holes in the cartoon drawing; from being the name of the powder, 'pounce' came to describe the process of tracing a design.

The first room to be tackled was the Staircase Hall. This part of the house was the most seriously damaged as it had acted as a chimney or funnel for the flames and thus drawn them away from the ground-floor rooms and prevented the external brickwork from being badly scorched or blackened. In the process almost all the ceiling plasterwork had been destroyed, but, remarkably, most of the mid-eighteenth-century plaster wall-panels on the east and west sides of the Hall still survived. The upper part of the outside

(north) wall incorporating Sir Matthew Fetherstonhaugh's mid-eighteenth-century Venetian window had collapsed. The ceiling had been a fine piece of rococo work, dating from Sir Matthew's first phase of internal re-modelling. It comprised a large irregular octagonal panel, with indented corners and a convex boss with scrolling foliage surrounded by shells and palm branches. The chunky gadrooned moulding round the octagon was run by Jacksons, but all the scrollwork and foliage were hand-modelled by Geoff Preston's Cliveden team. The boss was built up in layers and the small surviving portion of the original plaster was reincorporated; now it has been gilded, it is indistinguishable from the surrounding new work. The damaged wall-panels were also repaired by hand *in situ* by the Clive-den plasterers.

Although the Red Drawing Room had been relatively undamaged by the fire, the ceiling had collapsed and smashed into pieces. A substantial pro-portion of the rococo plasterwork had been salvaged during the post-fire archaeological dig. The fragments were all stripped of paint and proved to be in better condition than had been anticipated. The heads supporting baskets of fruit and flowers at either end of the room, though broken, were

Left: The ceiling designs were drawn up on polythene sheets and transferred to the flat beds of the ceilings by 'pouncing', pricking through the outlines of the drawing and dusting with powder. Anne King is working on the ceiling in the Red Drawing Room.

Right: Caspar Taylor, of Cliveden Conservation, hand-modelling the central plaster boss of the Staircase Hall ceiling, which was then regilded.

[83]

Restoration of the Red Drawing Room ceiling by Cliveden Conservation: (*above*) Diane Dollery laying out plaster fragments in the Miracle Span shed. This process was undertaken for each ceiling to establish the extent of surviving material, and to plan reinstatement; (*above right*) Anne King modelling missing elements in lime plaster; (*below right*) one of the plaster heads restored.

repaired and put back in their original positions. The centrepiece of loosely scrolling vine leaves and bunches of grapes also includes many original fragments. The basic framework of the ceiling, including the large irregular octagon with guilloche mouldings and the flanking rectangles with ribbon mouldings, were run by Jacksons. All the floral garlands and the cornucopiae of fruit were modelled free-hand by the Cliveden team. These decorations, together with the baskets of fruit, echo the carving of the white marble chimneypiece and contribute to the subtle unity of the room's design.

In the Little Drawing Room, many of the original plasterwork fragments were likewise incorporated in the reconstructed ceiling, including the central Apollo mask and one of the heraldic cartouches with the antelope crest of the Fetherstonhaughs, which Trevor Proudfoot had rescued intact

from the ruins four days after the fire. This room, like the Red Drawing Room, had also been surprisingly unscathed, even though the ceiling had been demolished by a falling chimneystack which took it and the boarded floor down into the basement below.

The Little Drawing Room before (*left*) and after the fire (*right*). A large section of the ceiling was retrieved and reinstated.

The unornamented ceiling in the adjoining Tapestry Bedroom had collapsed the morning after the fire (soon after the rescue of the Prince Regent's bed). The modillion cornice (of which a section survived intact) and the plain ceiling were both reinstated by Jacksons, who were also responsible for the plain ceiling of the Dining Room in the east range. In this latter room, the Cliveden Conservation Workshop copied the two plaster reliefs, and rectified the damage to four plaster busts by George Garrard commissioned by Sir Harry Fetherstonhaugh. Garrard, who had studied under the painter Sawrey Gilpin (whose daughter he married), was well known for his marble portrait busts and for his realistic small-scale reliefs of horses and cattle. Garrard's plaster plaques at Uppark (both dated November 1804) comprised a horse in a landscape inscribed 'The Wanton Courser' over the north door and a stag at bay over the south door. These plaques, inspired by Pope's translation of Homer, were seriously damaged in the fire; only a few sad remnants remained of the stag on the south wall (where the fire had been fiercest) and several elements of the northern horse, including its head, tail and foreleg. Because these fragments formed part of individual pieces of sculpture, rather than being decorative plaster-work, it was decided not to incorporate them (which would have been practically possible) but to make new copies. These were made by Richard Ireland and Louisa Pryor of the Cliveden Conservation Workshop. The original fragments are on display in the Uppark exhibition.

The replacement 'Garrard' plaques were made in the workshops at Cliveden. Apart from the original remnants, other sources for copying the reliefs were provided by a similar group of Garrard plaques (c.1805) over the entrance hall doors at Southill, in Bedfordshire, and by old photographs of the Uppark Dining Room. There was a 1941 *Country Life* view of the south wall, from which a blown-up detail showed the full form of the stag. The north plaque, with the horse, had been professionally photographed by the National Trust in 1974. Both photographs suffered from the inherent distortion caused by the angle from which they were taken and by the use of flashlights, but the surviving fragments, and comparison with the Southill plaques enabled these shortcomings to be overcome in the copies. The original remnants and the undamaged surface of Garrard's bust of Napoleon also allowed accurate paint analysis and the 'bronze' finish could therefore be precisely replicated by building up successive glazes, as originally.

Garrard's reliefs had been 'waste-moulded' in gypsum from clay reliefs that had been consumed in the process. The new reliefs were also cast in gypsum plaster, but this time from silicone rubber moulds. The retrieved pieces were used to make the casts and the lost sections sculpted in clay by Richard Ireland and Louisa Pryor. Garrard's reliefs, partially modelled in high relief, were virtuoso productions. The necks of the horse and stag, for instance, arched away from the ground of the plaques, and this dramatic depth of modelling has been most successfully achieved in the replicas. The opportunity was taken to reinstate the stag's outer antler, broken off long before the fire.

Garrard also supplied Sir Harry Fetherstonhaugh with four bronzed plaster busts of Whig worthies and heroes: Charles James Fox (1805), the 5th Duke of Bedford (1805), William Battine (1805) and Napoleon (1802). These stood on brackets in oval recesses on each side of the animal plaques at either end of the room, and were an integral part of its architecture. In the fire the bust of Fox had come off worst, with only one of his ears surviving; the Duke of Bedford was broken but repairable; Battine was water damaged and his complexion pock-marked; Napoleon was intact and only needed polishing. All three survivors were repaired, as necessary, and Fox was recast from a new model made by Louisa Pryor.

Richard Ireland also contributed to the restoration of the Little Parlour. This room, remodelled in *c.*1770, had a moulded lime plaster ceiling in the Adam manner which collapsed in the early hours of the morning of the fire. The principal features of the ceiling were four inserted oval medallions cast in gypsum. These were broken in pieces and the survival rate ranged from 20 per cent of the original in the worst case to 60 per cent in the case of the other three. The fragments were all transported to Cliveden and juggled about until they fitted together, with the right number of legs and arms allocated for each subject. They were then restored, with the missing pieces replaced in cast gypsum. In the process it was discovered that the originals were obviously composites, cast from different moulds; a

Restoration of the bronzed plaster bust of the 5th Duke of Bedford made by George Garrard in 1805: (*left*) fragments laid out ready for conservation; (*centre*) remodelling by Louisa Pryor, of Cliveden Conservation; (*right*) after repair and before painting to simulate bronze.

single plaque had several different perspective points and the modelling varied from the refined to the crude. One of the most fascinating aspects of the restoration of Uppark was the insight that was gained into original practices. Bodges and fudges were detected and it was possible to identify the hands of different craftsmen, including at least three who moulded the original ceilings. Once the gypsum plaques were put back, the garlands of husks and other decorative elements that linked them together were hand-modelled *in situ.* Jacksons cast the entire cornice, apart from an old section which survived to the left of the fireplace.

In the Saloon most of the decorative mural plasterwork survived the fire, although the ceiling itself had collapsed under the weight of fallen beams and masonry. It proved possible to bind the cornice back with wire, and

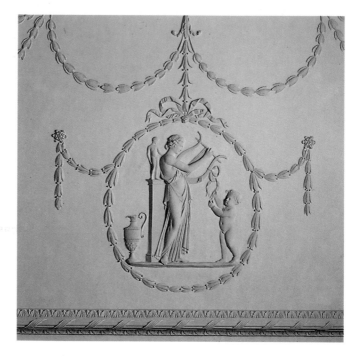

Restoration of one of the four gypsum plaster medallions from the Little Parlour ceiling, *c.*1770: (*above left*) remnants laid out to assess the survival rate; (*below left*) after conservation and restoration. The darker pieces represent the original plaster, the remainder was remodelled at Cliveden by Richard Ireland; (*right*) the medallion reinstated in the repainted ceiling.

some portions of the original coving were reincorporated in the new work. The bed of the ceiling was copied from the evidence previously marshalled by Richard Ireland during the laying-out of the surviving fragments. The setting-out of the elaborate Neo-classical design for this ceiling, the largest in the house, was by far the most complicated. The framework of the illusionistic coffered 'dome' in the centre was cast in small sections by Jacksons, as were the small circular fan ornaments in the diamond-shaped panels at either end. The floral *paterae* ranged in diminishing sizes in the coffers included many salvaged originals. The extensive scrollwork in the flanking panels was modelled by hand by the Cliveden team, as elsewhere. The surviving wall plasterwork needed only minor repair, although there were fears that dry rot might develop in the timber supporting the structure of the water-soaked plasterwork. The long-standing dry rot (caused by the inadequate cornice gutter above) in the south wall of the Saloon had largely consumed the laths and battens supporting the plaster walls, but it was eradicated by a combination of ventilation, the removal of defective timber and the application of fungicide to sound remaining wood. After the fire it was discovered that the Neo-classical urns and scrolls above the plaster picture frames on the north wall were complemented by similar decoration below, hidden when Repton's bookcases were installed in c.1815. Here the original green and white colour scheme had also survived undetected, having been replaced elsewhere in the room by Repton's white and gold décor.

The restoration of the Uppark plasterwork reflects the marriage of revived techniques with the conservation of surviving fragments and of archaeological and chemical analysis. The creative impetus has had wider benefits in the dissemination of the previously extinct craft of free-hand lime plaster, which has already been put to use in schemes elsewhere. Geoff Preston, for instance, has subsequently been responsible (this time under the umbrella of St Blaise) for the restoration of the fire-damaged Georgian plaster ceilings at Prior Park, in Bath; he is currently executing plasterwork in the United States. Others have worked in various National Trust properties including Mompesson House, in Salisbury. The Cliveden Conservation craftsmen are restoring some of Francis Bernasconi's fire-damaged stucco decorations (dating from 1829) at Windsor Castle; the plastering skills developed at Uppark are also relevant to architects designing new work in the classical manner.

The Uppark plasterwork was a unique and daunting project. Its successful completion was a notable first in this country and has established a high standard against which future plaster restoration will be measured. Many recall the excitement and spirit of endeavour in the early stages: it was, as Trevor Proudfoot put it, something to 'go for'. As confidence grew, it was mixed with a sense of surprise at the sheer gall of trying to reproduce work of such quality and beauty, and on such a scale.

5: Carving and Joinery

THE RESTORATION OF THE CARVING AND JOINERY in the principal ground-floor rooms at Uppark did not present so great a leap in the dark as the reconstruction of the ornamented stucco ceilings and wall decorations. A much greater proportion of the original woodwork had escaped the flames. Although the survival rate varied from room to room, perhaps 70 per cent of the eighteenth-century joinery was intact or repairable, amounting to over 5,000 individual sections and pieces. With

Left: The Little Drawing Room after the fire. Despite the obvious devastation, most of the original woodwork survived, as was the case in the majority of ground floor rooms.

Opposite: One of the serpent 'capitals' of the Saloon doorcases, *c.*1770, copied by Ben Harmes.

the exception of the main staircase, most of the work was largely a matter of cutting out and fitting in new, often quite small, sections and pieces where the old had been totally burnt or hopelessly charred.

Nor was there a shortage of qualified carvers and joiners capable of producing work of the highest quality and in the eighteenth-century spirit, although such craftsmen tended to be expensive. It could be argued that

English woodwork, from the Middle Ages to the present day, has been the pre-eminent national craft skill, comparable to marblework in Italy or stone-masonry in France. The English tradition of carved woodwork and high quality joinery has been unsurpassed for centuries, as is attested by the angel roofs, rood-screens and choir-stalls of the Middle Ages, the carvings of Grinling Gibbons in the seventeenth century or the glories of Georgian furniture. What was true of the past remains true today. Whereas the plaster-work at Uppark involved the resurrection of forgotten methods and a trawl for competent practitioners, there was a still living tradition of woodwork and a wide pool of experienced talent on which to draw.

After the fire, most of the surviving woodwork in the house was carefully dismantled, numbered and stored in controlled atmospheric conditions, while the structure of the building was repaired; only certain portions were protected *in situ*. The salvaged timber included the oak floorboards, panelled doors and shutters, carved architraves and fire surrounds, the panelling from the Dining Room, as well as previously hidden joinery such as the old timber wall-linings which incorporated the remains of the seven-teenth-century panelling and other Georgian salvage. Much of this wood-work was repaired in the workshops before reinstatement, and great care was taken to retain the old paintwork and gilding which had been one of the most distinctive ingredients of Uppark's untouched atmosphere.

Study of the internal joinery provided further historical evidence for the dating of the eighteenth- and early nineteenth-century alterations to the house. Most puzzling was the Dining Room, previously thought to be a survivor of the original seventeenth-century interior. But, as already men-tioned, the archaeological evidence confirmed the evidence of the 1705 inventory description and proved that the space was originally two rooms, with a partition about two-thirds of the way across. This indicated that a medium-sized room and a smaller room beyond had been knocked together. The materials and techniques of the surviving joinery also indi-cated that the room's appearance was the result of two phases of alterations: by Sir Matthew Fetherstonhaugh probably in *c.*1750 and by Sir Harry after 1810, when Humphry Repton merely altered an existing room for the latter. Repton installed the marble chimneypiece and the mirrored alcoves for the display of silver plate, introduced the bronzed plaster relief panels and busts by George Garrard and painted the room white and gold like the Saloon. Repton's alterations were partly executed in deal and plaster, whereas the rest of the joinery in the Dining Room, including the side wall panelling, the four giant fluted Corinthian pilasters on the end walls and the bold modillion cornice, was all of oak. The most likely explanation is that the room was made by Sir Matthew Fetherstonhaugh between 1747 and 1749, the probable date of his construction of a new kitchen and other service rooms in the partly sunken wings on the north side of the house. In the Dining Room he may have reused some seventeenth-century woodwork

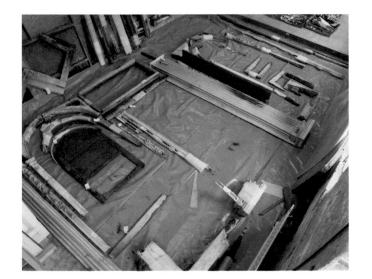

from the two earlier areas listed in the 1705 inventory, which would explain the room's slightly archaic character.

Examination of the timber throughout the ground floor revealed considerable reuse of the late seventeenth-century work. Panelling was often retained in Sir Matthew's mid-eighteenth-century remodelling as a lining beneath the new wall-coverings in the west range rooms, and the Little Parlour. Much of this groundwork was very simple in technique. While the visible surface mouldings were highly finished and the panelled doors properly and traditionally made with wedged through tenons, the timber wall-linings were usually crude, roughly axed to line and generally secured to the masonry either by wrought-iron hooks or nailed to small timber pieces driven into joints of the brickwork. There was little evidence of scribing or careful measurement, except for the occasional internal angle. Everything was nailed, with not a screw used in any of this joinery. All the wall-linings, except for the oak panelling in the Dining Room and the Little Parlour, were of deal or Baltic pine and were returned to their original positions after repair. Most of the fine carved work was also of Baltic pine, although some was executed in lime, a softer more malleable wood which responds well to the chisel. Lime had been much used for English architectural wood carving since the seventeenth century, when it was the favourite material of Grinling Gibbons and his school.

The floorboards throughout the ground floor were mainly of oak; they varied slightly in width, although most were over 8in (20cm) wide. The Dining Room and Little Parlour floors were of pine. All the floors had always been 'dry scrubbed' in the eighteenth-century manner, and not stained and polished. With their wide boards of inimitable silvery hue, they contributed enormously to the special quality of the interior. By a

Left: The remains of the panelling of the north wall of the Dining Room, laid out after the fire.

Right: The north wall restored and ready for painting and gilding, to match the surviving decoration.

The Red Drawing Room:
(*above*) the east wall
before the wallpaper was
hung, showing the
original wall-linings
repaired and reinstated;
(*below*) the room restored
and refurnished.

miracle, most of those on the ground floor survived the fire. They had been so well protected by the sludge of wet ash and fallen plaster that they were only singed here and there by the fall of burning beams, honourable scars thus being added to the patina of two centuries. The floorboards were loose tongued-and-grooved along the joints and 'secretly' dowelled together with wooden pegs at approximately 12-in (30-cm) intervals. They were either packed, with little wedges, or rabbeted with a thin strip of wood to the uneven floor joists, which were often of rough, reused timber. Each floorboard was marked with a grid reference before removal from the house so that after repair it could be returned to its precise location. The traditional methods of fixing were repeated.

It is, however, the decorative mural joinery, with its superlative carved enrichment, which catches the eye of the visitor. Unlike the rough and simple under-joinery, the Uppark carving is consistently of the highest quality. Its repair provided a rare opportunity for skilled modern crafts-

The Saloon: (*left*) section of one of the finely carved doorcases, *c.*1770, before the fire; (*right*) left undecorated after the fire to exhibit the extent of old and new carving.

men to pitch their capabilities against those of their eighteenth-century predecessors. Although they were struck by the quality of the work that they had to match, many little deceits and deceptions to trick the eye were found.

The work to be repaired or matched ranged from the robust but good quality oak capitals and swags in the Dining Room, through the highly competent fitting of the rococo west rooms, to the extraordinary peak of refinement in the Saloon and Little Parlour. Particularly fine were the

Saloon doorcases, with entwined snakes, delicate leaves and tendrils and exuberantly carved scrolls. In the mid-eighteenth-century work the carving was all cut out of the solid, but in the slightly later Saloon occasional elements were fretted out of lime and applied to the base with glue and fine pins.

Many of the original joinery techniques were highly sophisticated. Thus, in the concave arched heads of Repton's mirrored recesses in the Dining Room, the desired architectural effect was achieved by the composite use of curved, steamed, cut and laminated work. A glued veneer was also applied to the curved outline of the window pelmets in the Little Parlour. The wall sconces in the Saloon each comprised three wrought-iron armatures forming a base for the slender scrolling arms, whose carved wooden surfaces were applied in the form of a series of hollow limewood 'bobbins' threaded over the armatures, and mitred and glued before carving and oil gilding. All these complex techniques had to be emulated in the course of repair.

The National Trust's brief for the repair of the joinery was straightforward. All the surviving original work was to be kept and the new work incorporated to agreed cut lines, removing the minimum of the original consistent with economic repair. None of the old woodwork was to be stripped of paint or gilding, except where the surface was badly charred. A keen eye was kept on the work to make sure that nothing deemed capable of repair was lost. Even fire-damaged pieces were kept so long as the charring had not destroyed the original form. The brief precluded any cutting or extending of original material. Everything had to go back exactly as it had been. Once it had been proved that the reuse and retention of the old woodwork was usually cheaper than copying, the loss adjusters gave this approach their strongest support. The principal contractor for the joinery work was Ashby & Horner, one of the best joinery firms in the south-east, with workshops in Kent.

As with the plasterwork, the design panel, comprising the architects, the National Trust and the management contractor Lelliott, supervised the execution of the brief and the interviewing of prospective joiners and carvers. At the time, there were fears that there were insufficient carvers of quality to carry out the work, but such concerns proved unduly pessimistic. Once the contract was awarded, some fifty carvers were approached by the successful contractor. Each was asked to produce the same trial samples, comprising copies of a small section of a mid-eighteenth-century dado rail in deal and part of the Dining Room cornice in oak. Each was inspected by members of the panel, who were kept in ignorance of the identity of the carver, and was either approved or rejected. The results were surprising. Some of the foremost carvers in the country failed the test, while some barely known craftsmen excelled themselves. At least four of the carvers employed at Uppark were young apprentices who now produce high quality work in their own right.

The subcontract for all the carved woodwork in the ground-floor rooms, for repairing and laying the floorboards and for the joinery of the new staircase, was granted to St Blaise Ltd. Founded in 1980 by Ian Constantinides and based at Evershot, in Dorset, St Blaise had participated in a number of major conservation projects, including the repair of the garden buildings at Stowe, in Buckinghamshire. The company assembled a team of carvers from different backgrounds. Some came from the London building trade;

Michael Kemph, of St Blaise Ltd, restoring one of the Saloon candle sconces. Made of giltwood threaded over metal armatures, they proved particularly complicated to restore, and their exact shape had to be re-established by careful scrutiny of the photographic evidence.

others had worked for London and provincial antique dealers, who have helped to keep alive a tradition of native woodcarving by commissioning copies and repairs of the finest Georgian furniture. For instance, Ben Harmes, who restored the Saloon sconces, came from the London carving trade. Alan Lamb, who carved one of the damaged snakes and other missing sections of the Saloon doorcases as well as repairing and replacing carved furniture, had studied at the London College of Furniture, in Shoreditch; a baroque stringed-instrument maker by profession, he has since forsaken the lutes and viols for full-time virtuoso woodcarving.

What all these craftsmen had in common was a feeling for the period, and an aptitude for the accurate copying of eighteenth-century woodwork, although none had previously worked to such stringent requirements. Both the National Trust and the architects were seeking perfection, and even simple things were done and redone until they were absolutely right.

None of the restoration woodwork is an approximation; it is exact in every detail. Like artists who improve their technique by meticulously copying their predecessors, the craftsmen found working at Uppark an education in itself. Uppark was indeed an exhilarating experience in relation both to the scale of the project and to the quality of the work. The carvers were inspired by a mixture of fierce competition and mutual admiration of each other's work. Though not by nature gregarious – carvers are 'woodshed' men or women usually working in solitary workshops – they became accustomed to carving in a team, talking and mixing among themselves and the other trades. Part of the credit for this belonged to Andrew Townend, St Blaise's Site Manager, who was responsible for forging the unity of the disparate team. He was assisted by St Blaise's unflappable and extrovert young administrator, Jenny Lawrence, who acted as a social catalyst and ended up, in the words of one of the carvers, 'more or less running the work on site'.

The St Blaise carving and joinery team was divided in half. New joinery and runs of repetitive mouldings were produced in their workshops at Evershot; conservation of old material and smaller repairs were carried out on site in a purpose-built carpentry shed. For security reasons, no original woodwork was allowed to leave Uppark; pieces were repaired and trial assembled, and the carving registered and sent to the carver with a plaster cast. The replacements were produced with the ends left uncarved for finishing, final gluing and assembly at Uppark. Two of the carvers remained on site full time and were responsible for fixing the new work in place.

An important aspect of the conservation programme was the temporary environmental control of the storerooms, the joinery shop and the house itself while work proceeded. As soon as the shell was weathertight, the rooms were gently warmed with electric heaters and the humidity controlled and monitored. This was a source of irritation to the builders because it meant that doors, or temporary plastic flaps, had to be kept closed: as is well known, no free-born Englishman ever closes a door behind him if he can help it. Both the old timber and the new replacements were kept in identical conditions for a year before being permanently installed. The architects' specification required that all timber for new joinery should be purchased a year in advance and conditioned 'to achieve equilibrium with conserved material'. This ensured that when the woodwork was joined it did not crack or open up. Environmental control was an important factor in achieving a seamless restoration of the joinery; so far no cracks have appeared in the woodwork or on the plaster ceilings.

High priority was given to matching the quality of the original timber when choosing replacements. Modern timber is generally considered to be inferior to the deals imported from the Baltic for the English building trade in the eighteenth century. In fact, the original timber used at Uppark varied greatly in quality. It proved possible to make a good match by choosing slightly better than average quality timber from Messrs Lananton's ware-houses at Canary Wharf, in London, for the general joinery, with the best quality reserved for the carvers. A pragmatic approach was adopted in the case of the other materials used in the repair of the joinery. As well as the animal glues which had originally been used, some modern glues were employed. Instead of using catalysed epoxy wood consolidants to stabilise the retained but charred sections, Paraloid B72 was chosen because it does not have a permanent chemical impact. Stainless steel rather than iron was chosen for fixings, but nails rather than screws were used, as in the first place. Copies of eighteenth-century tools were made to help the carvers in their work. These small decisions were guided by common sense and prac-ticality, rather than by doctrinaire consistency.

The extent to which the joinery was copied or restored varied from room to room. As in the case of its plaster ceiling, the seventeenth-century Stair-case Hall joinery, which had suffered most in the fire, had to be replaced largely in replica, and incorporated only a few small fragments of the original. By comparison, the Saloon, Dining Room, Little Parlour and west range were largely conservation exercises, with much of the original wood-work still surviving and retaining its early nineteenth-century or Victorian paint finishes.

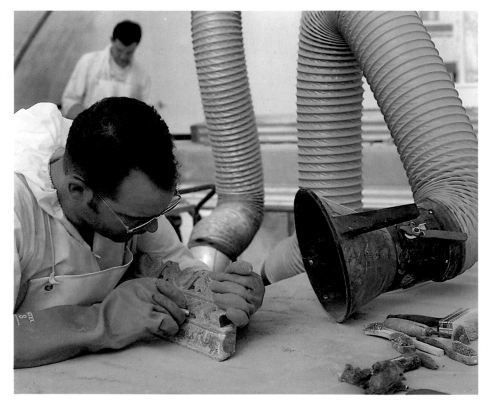

Charred or irrevocably damaged paint was removed from decorative woodwork by chemical treatment followed by vacuum cleaning in controlled conditions.

In the Staircase Hall, all that remained of the seventeenth-century staircase, a survival from Lord Tankerville's interior, was a section of newel, a few balusters, a couple of treads, stumps of the carriage and small sections of the handrail. The incorporation of these scanty fragments was a condition of the contract for the new staircase. The new design is an accurate copy of the original stair, but the patina and texture, acquired over centuries of wear as well as by the application and removal of paint at various stages in its history, proved impossible to match. The new polished wood has something of the appearance of Edwardian luxury neo-Georgian joinery. It has proved perhaps the most controversial aspect of the restoration of Uppark and is the one significant element of the state rooms which the SPAB still considers should have been replaced by a 'new design'.

The new stairs are built of English oak, with three wide flights and two quarter landings on a traditional carriage of five pieces, supported at the quarter landings by posts hidden within the panelling. The handrail is chunky and almost square in section; it is ramped at the ends, and constructed of laminated timber, whereas the original was all in one piece. The barley-sugar balusters are a *tour de force* of the turner's art, in that the barley-twist diminishes in pitch, throat and diameter as it rises. The old balusters were all hand-carved, but the new ones were turned on a specially adapted lathe by Messrs Cherry & Co. of Martock, in Somerset, then finished by hand. The construction is a triumph of the joiner's craft, the balusters and each tread and riser being ingeniously and invisibly dovetailed into place.

Brian Fowler of St Blaise, who was responsible for its setting-out, gloried in its complications. Even though lines on the plasterwork provided evidence for the rise of the seventeenth-century staircase, many irregularities were found and all had to be incorporated in the new design if the stair were to fit the well exactly. Thus, each flight has a slightly different rising. Many compromises and tricks of construction reflect the fact that Lord Tankerville's craftsmen had erected their staircase without the benefit of accurate site dimensions and had played it by eye as they went along. None of this is immediately obvious, but once grasped it adds to one's appreciation of the new staircase.

The staircase was manufactured in St Blaise's Dorset workshops, with modern equipment used to size up but traditional tools to finish. The secret dovetails were all made by hand. While the finish is all in the traditional manner, the structure included a number of modern elements as well as the use of laminated timber. The bearers for the treads were bolted, rather than nailed as originally, to the sides of the carriage pieces, which, like their predecessors, were also bolted together. Apart from the laminated areas, however, all the joinery is dry-jointed in the traditional manner without the use of glue. A trial assembly of the sections took place in the workshop before transportation of the staircase to Uppark, where fortunately it fitted perfectly.

The Staircase Hall: (*above left*) the day after the fire. Almost all the seventeenth-century bolection moulded panelling in the lower hall and most of the staircase were destroyed; (*above right*) the foot of the staircase before the fire. Constructed *c.*1690 in oak, it was probably originally painted white and gold, grained to simulate oak in 1826, and, as shown in this photograph, stripped of its paint in 1933–4; (*below left*) the new staircase in course of construction by St Blaise Ltd; (*below right*) old and new joinery clearly discernible at the foot of the stairs and in the landing balustrade.

The repair of the Dining Room panelling, on the other hand, presented a puzzle of fitting in new pieces into substantial areas of original work. Over 50 per cent of the old joinery had survived, including the panelling on the side walls, some of the modillion cornice and large fragments of the Corinthian set-piece on the north wall; the south wall had been largely burnt. All the woodwork was removed from the room for repair, and new pieces were carved in oak to match. The splendid Corinthian capitals and carved swags flanking the arched recesses on the north wall were the work of Derek Medway. Fitting it all together again in the room entailed repeated juggling and rearrangement. The worst problem was that the new ceiling was an inch too low and the Corinthian pilasters would not quite fit. Since an inch could not be sawn off the pilasters, the ceiling, which fortunately had not yet been plastered, had to be adjusted to leave the correct clearance. Then the window shutters would not fit, so the whole of that wall had to be dismantled and the panelling reassembled. And so it continued – 'half an inch to the left, no, a quarter of an inch to the right' – until it all finally clicked into place and the sigh of relief could be heard in South Harting.

In the Little Parlour and the Saloon tiny repairs were made to damaged carvings and missing sections were carefully fitted into place. Those who saw these rooms before they were painted and papered were impressed by the almost miraculous piecing in of an arabesque here, a snake's head there or a short piece of perfectly matching egg-and-dart; the hand of the modern carver was revealed only in the still raw natural wood. Now that the mends are painted over they are invisible, except for one or two small sections that have been left bare to illustrate the carvers' skills and the careful patching which has taken place.

In the Tapestry Bedroom, the carved wooden chimneypiece has been given a new shelf, and a few missing curls in the carving have been neatly replaced. That many of these piecing-in repairs are the work of different hands is the result of an internal tendering system for every portion of the work, the most appropriate carver being chosen in each case. Although it is copy-work, the hands are slightly different and this gives variety and life to the new work just as it did to the eighteenth-century carving now known to have been the product of at least three different craftsmen. Thus, the writhing snakes' heads terminating the scrolls on either side of the west doorcase in the Saloon are by different carvers: the right-hand head is by Alan Lamb and that on the left by Ben Harmes. It is an interesting test to see if the untutored eye can spot the difference.

At the very beginning of the restoration project, in November 1989, the National Trust had announced: 'For the ground-floor rooms, there will be no guesswork. With the records we can get it exactly right, incorporating the large amount of existing material we have saved.' In relation to the joinery this forecast was more than accurate. A much larger proportion of

One of the window embrasures in the Saloon, showing the refinement of the original carving, and the subtlety with which it has been emulated in the repairs.

The Tapestry Room chimneypiece, *c.*1750, before the fire (*right*) and during repair (*above*). A new shelf and several minor additions were required, but otherwise it survived intact, and the original elements did not require repainting or regilding.

the eighteenth-century fabric was incorporated than was at first thought feasible, with the result that the restored rooms at Uppark are totally convincing. Only the staircase has emerged unintentionally as a frank copy, but it seems no more out of place than, for example, Romaine Walker's brilliant Edwardian neo-baroque staircase, with its reproduction of a Tijou iron balustrade, in the Painted Hall at Chatsworth, in Derbyshire, or Francis Johnson's 1960s copy of Carr of York's cantilevered mahogany staircase at Everingham, in Yorkshire, to mention two country houses enhanced by the insertion of a twentieth-century replica staircase, although, mercifully, not as a result of fire damage.

6: Paint and Decoration

BEFORE 1989, UPPARK REPRESENTED the ideal English house. Its comparatively small size was in its favour, and its exterior, mellowed brick with stone dressings, in the homely Anglo-Dutch style of the late seventeenth century, comfortably suggested a doll's-house. As early as 1910, *Country Life* pronounced that Uppark had 'escaped alteration in a wonderful degree' and, in 1941, the architectural historian Christopher Hussey in the same magazine described its antiquarian atmosphere, 'as delicate and fragrant as the bloom on a grape'. He continued: 'It is the kind of house where you feel that you might look through the window into the life of another age' and he felt that its romantic history was suggested and enhanced by the fading and ageing of 'silks and paint impregnated with light streaming in through two score great windows for so long'. As Hussey explained, 'the untouched perfection of Uppark' was largely due to the curious circumstances of Sir Harry Fetherstonhaugh's longevity and of his unusually late and childless marriage to a farmer's daughter, fifty years his junior. Thus Uppark became 'the bower of Sleeping Beauty for a hundred and twenty years', being cherished largely unchanged by Sir Harry's widow and by her unmarried sister until 1895, when it was inherited by Turnour-Fetherstonhaughs and Meade-Fetherstonhaughs who respected the Uppark tradition of preservation. Christopher Hussey went on to describe Admiral and Lady Meade-Fetherstonhaugh's careful husbandry in the 1930s: 'tattered, sun-rotted curtains have been darned from head to foot by the ladies of the house almost where they hung, their faded crimson brought to life again by lotions of *Saponaria*; the colours of carpets and *petit point* nursed back to life. This ten years' labour of love is the latest chapter, and not the least wonderful in the fairy tale'.

Hussey might also have mentioned Lady Meade-Fetherstonhaugh's preference for touching up rather than renewing old paint and wallpapers, and her precocious sense that Uppark should be treated with the subtle hand of a conservator rather than with the zeal of a restorer. That the article was written in 1941 must have inspired his musings on what Uppark represented. In the year after the Battle of Britain, the future was uncertain:

Allyson McDermott fixing a section of salvaged wallpaper into its former place in the Red Drawing Room. Original fragments were set into the new paper, which was matched for colour at the printing stage and toned with watercolour *in situ* to camouflage the joins.

In these days to be privileged to tread the short crisp turf of Uppark and muse in those exquisite rooms, so happy and so historic, is to steep every sense in England's *ichor*, distilled from her soil, her climate, her history and art. Love and care are the spell that have so magically preserved this precious and irreplaceable home.

Hussey ended by quoting Lady Meade-Fetherstonhaugh's own description of the great house at that time:

At night, when the wind blows over the down, there is as of old the sound of drumming hoofs – the throbbing drone of enemy bombers over the dark silent land. The challenging bark and roar of England's coast guns stir echoes at Uppark of war and threatened invasions lurking in dark corners of its history, notes of an unfinished symphony that time plays slowly out within these sun-baked, storm-washed walls.

The Saloon: (*above left*) the north-east corner in 1941. According to the *Country Life* writer, Christopher Hussey, Uppark's interiors had 'escaped alteration in a wonderful degree', representing the quint-essence of eighteenth-century decoration; (*above right*) the central door in the north wall after the fire. Although the paint and gilding were untouched, fire-water and exposure had increased its former fading. It was left un-restored and taken as a model for adjacent sections of new decoration; (*below*) the north wall after restoration. The flat plaster was redecorated to match the surviving white and gold decor, *c.*1815. The green paint revealed behind the pictures represents the original scheme of *c.*1770.

The decision to repair Uppark after the 1989 fire committed the Trust to the revival of this long tradition of care, good housekeeping and loyalty to the past. The principle that Uppark should be restored to its previous state 'insofar as that is practicable' served as a reliable sheet-anchor in establishing a policy for the repair of Uppark's interior decoration. Only occasionally, as in the repainting of Repton's north entrance corridor, was this strategy contravened, in this case to return to Repton's original stone colour found beneath the 1970s pink, thus reversing an earlier National Trust scheme, which had not followed historic precedent. The overall aim has been to provide an appropriate setting for the contents of the principal rooms, the majority of which had been rescued almost unscathed. Salvaged curtains and carpets and faded gilding on furniture, picture and mirror frames would have looked dowdy in overtly new surroundings redecorated with bright new paint and with untoned gold leaf. The visual unity for which Uppark had been renowned would have been lost.

There were, none the less, several choices: either Uppark would look much as it had before; or the interior would look unashamedly new, with no attempt to tie in the new with the old (the original colours would be established and the rooms redecorated to illustrate their initial state); or, a third possibility, a patchwork of old and new would be left so that the difference could readily be appreciated. There was, in fact, a moment before the rooms were partially redecorated, when it was possible to discern fragments of plaster and sections of coving replaced in their origi-nal positions. It was fascinating while the rooms were empty, and was recorded and photographed in great detail, but it would have looked bizarre with the contents reinstalled. It seemed far more logical that Uppark should re-emerge from its ordeal with its appearance as unaltered as possible and that the collection should once more live in harmony with its surroundings. The rooms would bear evident scars, but, provided a comprehensive record was kept of the process of repair, the extent of the

The south wall of the Saloon before the fire, showing painting and gilding, *c.*1815, touched up but never wholly redecorated subsequently (see p.103).

damage could be communicated by photographs, film, diagrams and so on.

Having repaired the interiors, the easiest option would have been to redecorate wholesale rather than to conserve surviving paintwork and gilding. The preservation of repairable and undamaged painted and gilded surfaces, made more friable by heat and water, posed a greater challenge. Why make the attempt? There were several reasons for preferring conservation to wholesale redecoration. The first was that the repair of Uppark was intended to be quite literal. Conservation of existing fabric was the guiding principle, and replacement was only considered acceptable when gaps could be filled in no other way. There was every reason not to exclude decorative surfaces from this consistent approach. In addition, Uppark's long tradition of preservation in preference to change had been continued by the National Trust since 1954, when it assumed the mantle of the donor family. As early as 1829, gilding was being repaired rather than replaced, and in 1831 paintwork was cleaned rather than repainted. Just as Lady Meade-Fetherstonhaugh in the 1930s had avoided redecoration by carefully touching up old paint, so the Trust – with the advice of the decorator John Fowler, the Trust's consultant on interior decoration – had generally limited its attentions to repainting and regilding shutters and window embrasures which had been bleached by sunlight.

In the 1970s, the walls and ceiling of the Little Parlour and the whole of the North Corridor and Staircase Hall were redecorated following visitors' complaints about the tattiness of the house. The fire provided an opportunity to rethink. Even in particularly damaged rooms such as the Little Parlour, where repainting *in extenso* was inevitable, areas where the original paintwork had survived were left alone (even when they were only 1970s retouchings on dados and door architraves). The result looks patchy, but is in accord with established maintenance practice before the fire and the patchiness has been mitigated by the reintroduction of pictures and furniture. In these scarred rooms, an impression of continuity is created by the reinstatement of conserved water-gilded fillet in its original position around the borders of the walls, so that the abrasion of housemaids' regular dusting at a low level continues to contrast with better preserved gilding higher up. A similar effect is produced by the relaid oak floorboards, which retain their dry-scrubbed appearance although they are now spattered with burn marks. In the Staircase Hall, the only room with a polished floor (comparatively recent), the polish was removed by heat and water. It was not renewed.

The seventeenth-century bolection panelling in the Staircase Hall was almost totally destroyed. Here, and in most other rooms, the new panelling was painted with lead paint as it would have been before the introduction of modern paints in the 1970s. The type of paint and the sequence of

The North Corridor: (*left*) before the fire as redecorated by John Fowler in the 1970s; and (*right*) after the fire with Repton's original early nineteenth-century stone colour restored.

colour schemes was established by microscopic paint analysis. Where lead-based paint was reapplied, it was built up, following the original method, in a sequence of coats, and 'flatted' to dull it down. This process is often described in the early nineteenth-century housepainters' bills. In 1826, the Venetian window and cornice of the Staircase Hall were 'twice flatted Dead White', while the walls were 'flatted Peach Blossom Colour', a picturesque description of the pale pink.

The almost completely new oak staircase in the Staircase Hall presented a problem. In 1826, the oak stair, which may originally have been white and gold, was 'Grained in imitation of New Oak'. It was stripped in the 1930s by Lady Meade-Fetherstonhaugh when Sir Harry Fetherstonhaugh's name was found scratched on the graining of the handrail. Not all the paint had been removed from the crevices, and this adventitious patchiness, still evident in the surviving fragments that had been incorporated, could not be reproduced after the fire. Regraining the new oak might perhaps have been a more successful means of tying it in with the reinstated original sections of the balustrade. At present, the new wood has a rather unsatisfactory smooth and polished appearance, especially in relation to the incorporated original wood and to the floorboards at the foot of the stairs. In the future, it is possible that some adjustment to its appearance may have to be made.

The new lead paint, mixed specially for Uppark to an authentic recipe by Hirst Conservation Ltd, was pre-aged so that after application it should not continue to darken naturally with the passage of time. This reduced the contrast between adjacent areas of new and old paintwork. The use of lead paint reflected the principle that original materials and methods should be used in the repair of Uppark. This approach had to be modified, however, in the case of the Saloon and Dining Room, where much of the original decoration was conserved and where patching with lead paint proved to be visually unacceptable. Accordingly, white lead paint applied in c.1815 and faded to a powdery grey in the Saloon, or cream in the Dining Room, was imitated with a more stable casein paint (based on milk).

Another difficulty was presented by the newly plastered ceilings. In the eighteenth and early nineteenth centuries, it was a standard practice to distemper new plaster ceilings, thus allowing rooms to be lived in while the moisture in the plaster gradually evaporated through a porous paint surface. When the plaster was solid and the hardening process complete, the distemper was washed off and replaced, if required, with lead-based oil paint and with gilding. In 1764, the builders of Spencer House, in London, 'were very unlucky in their weather for the drying of the ceiling which will have delayed the gilding a little but that will be only of a few days'. At Uppark, dehumidification for more than a year had encouraged the natural process of drying. It was still impossible to risk the use of an impervious lead paint, but since applying distemper as a first stage and

The east wall of the Staircase Hall before the fire, showing the effect of stripping the paint from the staircase balustrade in the 1930s.

The Saloon: (*left*) immediately after the fire. Despite the fall of the ceiling and the collapse of the temporary roof in early 1990, much of Repton's white and gold decoration was preserved; (*right*) revealed behind Repton's bookcases was the second decorative scheme of green and white (see p.115).

then washing it off would have been impractical, a special porous modern paint was used that had the appearance of flatted lead. So far, there has been no flaking of paint or loss of gilding on the ceilings, all of which were renewed incorporating a greater or lesser volume of original fragments.

The individual histories of the state rooms reveal how these principles were adopted in practice. Roger White, then Secretary of the Georgian Group, anticipated the Trust's approach in 1990:

A building that has been allowed to grow old gracefully has a certain magic, almost indefinable quality, which we tend to label 'patina'. Where patina survives it is something to be cherished and protected .... when it is gone, however, it cannot be artificially recreated, and one simply has to wait for the building to grow old again. This will be the case at Uppark.

The mural decoration of the Saloon had survived the fire largely undamaged, but underwent a second ordeal following the collapse of Uppark's temporary roof in the gale of January 1990. The fact that the house was then open to the elements for six months, beginning with the most inclement season of the year, explains why much of the Saloon paint was found to be friable and unsound. None the less, a high proportion of original paint, and an even higher level of original gilding, was conserved; the remainder was discreetly toned in to match. Some areas, for example, the paint and gilding of the relief plasterwork, Repton's bookcases and the doorcase between them, were left virtually untouched, even if they were more faded and

The Saloon, restoration complete.

'washed out' than before the fire. The aim was minimal intervention to preserve the appearance of the room as it had been – shabby, but in keeping with its faded contents, the whole forming, without exaggeration, one of the most beautiful *ensembles* in England.

Paint analysis by Catherine Hassall of University College, London, and Patrick Baty, owner of Papers and Paints Ltd of London, confirmed the Saloon's reputation as a room which had not been decorated since the early nineteenth century. It was painted white and gold by Humphry Repton, when he introduced the pair of bookcases flanking the north door in *c*.1815. When these were removed, after the fire, for protection and conservation, decorative plasterwork continuing that on the plaster picture frames above was discovered. This revelation confirmed the evidence of paint analysis and proved that the Saloon had been decorated twice before *c*.1815.

The original scheme of *c*.1770 was the most elaborate: a dark green for the walls (still evident behind the pictures in architectural plaster frames) was relieved by the stony white of the raised plasterwork and woodwork; the ceiling compartments were in alternating lavender and blue, again with white picking-out. The second scheme of between *c*.1770 and *c*.1815

Gilding the Saloon ceiling. After completion, the gold leaf was toned to match surviving patinated gilding, but with brighter highlights, as before the fire.

(revealed by the plasterwork behind Repton's bookcases) consisted of paler green walls, again picked out in white, with a pink and white ceiling. Repton's décor of white and gold (which no doubt reflected Sir Harry's Francophile taste) was originally based on the brightest and most expensive white, faded over the years to a soft grey. It is extremely rare for a room to have retained its decoration for nearly 200 years and this in itself would have prompted an attempt to preserve rather than repaint. The accounts presented by Charles Pepper, a London housepainter, reveal that the gilding was repaired in 1829 and that in 1831, the 'Walls & Wood' of the Saloon and Staircase Hall underwent 'Scowering & Cleaning'. In 1859, twelve years after Sir Harry's death, another London firm, Thomas Harland 'House and decorative painters, paper hangers etc', confined its attentions to 'the sashes in the Saloon', and this type of conservative maintenance continued until the fire.

Fortunately, most of the contents of the Saloon were rescued soon after the fire was discovered, and although the fixed pictures were taken down at

a more hazardous stage, major surgery was not necessary. The only serious losses (no longer noticeable) were one curtain with its parcel-gilt Neo-classical pelmet and the partial immolation of the west doorcase, where one of the architraves in the form of a writhing snake has been left un-decorated to show the piecing together of conserved and replacement carving. The picture-hang, like the décor, has remained unaltered since at least *c.*1820, when a diagram first recorded not only the fixed pictures installed *c.*1770 but also the two pairs of Zuccarellis and Batonis which hang from picture rails on yellow plaited silk cords matching the curtains, as in Repton's Dining Room.

Whereas Repton's alterations to the Saloon are fully documented, responsibility for the room's original design remains uncertain. As we have seen, the most likely candidate is James Paine, the architect of Sir Matthew's town house, although Christopher Hussey, while allowing the possibility, was inclined to advocate the claims of Henry Keene, who completed the Gothick so-called 'Vandalian Tower' in the park in 1776. Coved and

The Dining Room looking south, in about 1965. The room was decorated in white and gold by Repton between 1812 and 1814, and left largely untouched thereafter.

compartmented ceilings were, however, characteristic of Paine at this date, as, for example, at Sandbeck Park, in Yorkshire, Brocket Hall, in Hertfordshire, and Shrubland Park, in Suffolk, and his previous connection with Sir Matthew is an argument for his authorship. The earlier Kentian chimneypieces (*c*.1750), consistent with Paine's earlier style, must represent the first stage of Sir Matthew's alteration of the original Great or 'Marble Hall'.

As in the Saloon, the fire spared substantial amounts of paint and gilding in the Dining Room, whose decoration, like that of the Saloon, was created by Repton and not redone since. The original lead-based oil paint, presumably applied soon after Thomas and James Hughes were paid for plasterwork in 1812–13, was of a warmer tone than the bright white of the Saloon, and has faded to cream rather than bluish grey. The missing paint was again replaced in casein, since a satisfactory match was impossible to achieve in lead paint. The north and south walls, with Corinthian pilasters flanking a central double door, and mirrored alcoves to either side, were most badly damaged, although the south wall was in a far worse state than at the north end, where the fire was less fierce. At both ends, and on the south pier, redecoration was the only option. On the fireplace wall, however, and on the northerly pier of the window wall, about 70 per cent of the

The Dining Room after the fire: (*above*) looking south after restoration and repainting; (*below*) the fireplace (west) wall before partial redecoration. Even the shadows of the picture hang, *c.*1820, can be seen on the original paint. The pictures have since been returned to their old places.

original paint and gilding survived so that the shadows of the picture-hang recorded in a set of diagrams of *c.*1820 were clearly discernible. The pictures, including the group of four landscapes by Joseph Vernet acquired in Rome in 1751, have been returned to their original positions on panelling that, after gentle cleaning, is shabbier than before the fire but none the less extensively retains much of its original surface treatment. Given that the furniture and textiles also survive, this has proved to be one of the two most convincing of the repaired interiors. As in the Saloon, paint conservation and partial redecoration was subtly achieved by Hirst Conservation Ltd. The glass in the alcoves has been replaced with nineteenth-century glass acquired through the antiques trade, but only one of the marble slabs beneath has had to be replaced – a disused quarry near Carrara in northern Italy was reopened for the purpose.

Repton took great pains over the alteration and redecoration of the Dining Room and of the new adjacent Servery. In October 1813, Repton was considering papering the Dining Room panels and ceiling with a 'Network of twisted rope – the size of my finger – ... in Garter blue rope on yellow ground'. Blue and yellow were to be taken up by the window curtains, and a blue velvet curtain was also recommended for the stained-glass Servery window, while the Dining Room alcoves were to have 'a drapery of Garter blue velvet with gold fringe which might be very magnificent in contrast with the Gold Plate'. Sir Harry's widow inherited, according to the 1874 inventory, no less than 12,032oz of Dining Room silver and silver gilt, so the intention to create a display on 'Plate racks' within the alcoves would have been comparable to the Prince Regent's practice at Carlton House, in London, and in the Brighton Pavilion.

Sir Harry finally settled on plain yellow curtains and on 'Looking Glasses in the recesses', chosen carefully for their clarity. Oil lamps were supplied to multiply the reflections by night and light effects 'both by day and candlelight' were also considered for the stained glass in the Servery. Repton anticipated that 'the effect will be magic as all the light may proceed from this Window with Argand Lamps properly adjusted behind'. With both pairs of double doors opened at either end of the Dining Room, the stained glass in the Servery was reflected in the overmantel glass of the Stone Hall, and the effect, combined with the infinite reflections of silver and candlelight in the four alcove mirrors, must indeed have been magical.

A pair of ebony and ivory sideboard cabinets, inlaid with panels of *pietre dure*, which stood on the piers, was added to the existing eighteenth-century leather upholstered mahogany dining-room furniture. Incinerated upstairs in 1989 in the family dining-room, these represented Sir Harry's most fashionable furniture commission; similar pieces were bought by the Prince Regent from the London firm of Marsh & Tatham for Carlton House. Their design may have been due to Charles Heathcote Tatham (1772–1842), brother of the furniture-maker Thomas, a scholarly Neo-classical architect who, after Repton's death in 1818, assumed a similar position in Sir Harry's affections.

Despite the fire, the Dining Room and Servery remain the principal testament to Sir Harry's friendship and collaboration with the leading landscape architect of the day. Both Sir Harry and Repton thought that

Uppark was built by Inigo Jones – it is not impossible that the white and gold colour scheme introduced here by Repton was intended to allude to Jonesian seventeenth-century interiors. Sir Harry's prominent placing of the portraits of Sir Cuthbert and Lady Fetherstonhaugh, his Elizabethan forebears, alongside Garrard's busts of Whig notabilities and of Napoleon, the reviver of the decorative arts of France, indicates something of a memorialising intention. The careful restoration of the room, preserving as much of Repton's décor as possible, is therefore in keeping with his original concept.

Like the Saloon and the Dining Room, the Red Drawing Room retains much of its original wall decoration, this time in the form of flock wall-paper. Torn down *in extremis* by the firemen, its restitution has made a significant contribution to the seemingly unaltered aspect of the room. Already in 1941, 'the old wallpapers ... were well saved yet falling apart'. The wallpaper here and upstairs was assumed to be eighteenth-century (the upstairs Blue Drawing Room paper was indeed so), no doubt because of its ancient and battered appearance, faded from crimson (still evident behind the pictures and pier-glasses) to a warm reddish brown. The fire revealed, however, that the crimson damask flock (previously considered by experts to be mid-nineteenth-century) had been laid over a much earlier (and undoubtedly mid-eighteenth-century) crimson flowered flock, made at a time when English flock papers were renowned for their superior quality of manufacture.

In 1748, the painter-stainer Thomas Bromwich was paid £45 16s by Sir Matthew, presumably for wallpaper. The earlier paper seems directly comparable to the contemporary 'Flower'd Red Paper' (since replaced by silk) of the Drawing Room at Felbrigg, the National Trust property in Norfolk, originally supplied during Paine's alterations (1751–6) for William Windham. This discovery of the Red Drawing Room's original flock paper, designed as at Felbrigg as a foil to Old Master pictures, pro-vides another clue to the probable responsibility of Paine for Sir Matthew's first phase of alterations at Uppark. The replacement paper was supplied either in 1851 or 1859 when the London craftsmen Henry Piper of Eastcheap and Thomas Harland of Southwark presented bills for red, crimson and satin wallpapers. The 'drawing room' hung in 1859 could well have been this room, and these accounts confirm that such renewals formed part of the generally conservative treatment of Uppark following Sir Harry's death in 1846.

By contrast to the salvage of the wallpaper, and of the majority of the water-gilded wallpaper fillet which was returned to its original positions, most of the paintwork has been renewed since the fire and this has compromised the room's otherwise shabby appearance. With the collapse of the ceiling, it was impossible to preserve its decoration, another remark-able survival from the early nineteenth century. This blue and white scheme (rather than the original plain white) was repeated, but the paint is in uneasy contrast to the battered and faded wallpaper.

The conservation of the wallpaper after the fire was extremely complicated. First, the salvaged paper underwent emergency conservation to surface-clean and stabilise it before it was placed in temporary storage in a controlled environment at Petworth House. This initial process was specified by Mary Goodwin, then the Trust's adviser on paper conservation, and undertaken by Orde Solomons, a freelance paper conservator who has specialised in the treatment of wallpaper. Before further cleaning and studio repair, the surviving elements, incorporating large pieces from the east and west walls and hundreds of smaller fragments (charred to a greater or lesser degree and with different tones of fading and therefore of colour) were laid out to establish their original positions. This was carried out at Petworth by Allyson McDermott, a paper conservator and wallpaper specialist whose firm had won the tender. With the aid of pre-fire photographs and by careful scrutiny of the colour changes, a giant jigsaw puzzle gradually disclosed the correct location of most fragments. Those impossible to place were used for patching. Clues were provided by the unfaded crimson rectangles behind pictures and mirrors, and border pieces were identified by the unfaded lines left by the gilt fillet below the cornice and above the dado, around architraves and fireplaces and set vertically in the room's corners.

After surface-cleaning with sable brushes and a filtered vacuum, the wallpaper pieces were interleaved with acid-free tissue paper and rolled on to padded tubes for transport to Allyson McDermott's conservation studio in County Durham. There, loose flock and flaking adhesive were consolidated. Old lining canvas and papers were removed and, after de-acidification (by water treatment) and repair, the original fragments were relined on to a conservation quality rag paper with a purified starch paste.

The next challenge for Allyson McDermott and her colleagues was the reproduction of the wallpaper into which the original fragments were eventually to be set. The reproduction paper was made following analysis of the composition and method of manufacture of the original. Hot-pressed wove paper, in a continuous roll, was used as a support. Several shades of wool flock were manufactured at Rose Mill, Oldham, in Lancashire – one batch to match the brownish colour of the faded flock, another to match the original crimson, and another undyed. These were mixed in various proportions depending on the location of the reproduction paper within the room. Fibre length was also important and numerous experiments had to be carried out to achieve an accurate copy. Traditionally, wallpaper was printed by hand with a hardwood block of pear or cherry, chosen for their close grain. Mahogany was selected in this case because the damask pattern was not particularly precise and mahogany is far easier to carve. The carving method, based on Robert Dossie's *Handmaid to the Arts* (1764),

The Red Drawing Room, east wall (detail), a photograph taken in the mid-1960s and showing unfaded rectangles of wallpaper which had been previously protected by the picture hang of *c*.1820, repeated when the wallpaper was replaced in the 1850s.

involved pricking through the design from a drawing backed with red chalk which was stuck to the mahogany block. Once transferred, the pattern was carved by hand using carving chisels and a wooden mallet.

Analysis revealed that the crimson was made up of carmine pigment bound up in animal glue, with a top layer of translucent varnish to improve both the depth of colour and the adhesion of the flock. Adjustments had to be made to simulate the deterioration and fading of the original varnish. Carmine was used to reproduce the unfaded areas, but ochres and umbers were required to suggest the much more general fading of the original. Special brushes, based on those reproduced in old manuals, were made so that the ground colours could be laid on exactly as they had been originally. First, a large rectangular brush covered the surface of the paper with pigment; then the uniform appearance of the original ground was achieved by working over the surface with a circular brush. Next came the printing of the damask pattern on to the ground. An ink trough was filled with the coloured adhesive, originally made up of a toxic lead compound and linseed oil as well as pigment. Modifications were made to conform to modern health and safety standards. The block was pressed into the mixture, then applied to the paper, a press being used to achieve a uniform pressure over the whole back of the block. Areas that had not taken were filled in with a brush afterwards. Block-printing each section of a length by hand makes it difficult to lay down the pattern in a straight line. This, and the slight variations of pressure from one application of the block to

another results in an attractive irregularity which is one of the hallmarks of hand-blocked wallpaper. With flock wallpaper, the woollen flock is sprinkled on to the paper after the pattern has been printed with the coloured adhesive and then pressed down. In the past, wallpaper manufacturers ingested clouds of flock, and presumably died of 'wallpaper maker's lung'. Accordingly, the Uppark flock was laid on in controlled conditions, with the workers being protected by special clothing, breathing apparatus and an extraction system.

Before paper hanging, the Red Drawing Room walls, lined as before the fire with recycled panelling, were first covered with conservation grade linen, rather than with the original coarse hessian seamed horizontally and backed around the edges. Lining paper, closely matching the weave of the original, was then stuck down with modern conservation adhesives rather than starch paste and animal glue. Reproduction wallpaper, varying in colour depending on location, was then hung. The original conserved fragments were set into this in their original positions, where these were known. When all the pieces of original paper had been applied, the new paper visible in the gaps between was toned *in situ* with conservation pigments brushed on by hand so as to disguise the joins.

The result looked convincing even before the pictures and pier-glasses were hung; afterwards it is hardly possible to tell the difference between pre- and post-fire decoration. By conserving and reapplying the original paper, all the eccentric variations of colour and tone due to fading are present once again. Water-staining around the fireplace (due to old leaks) has probably been exacerbated by the water from the fire hoses, but this increases a sense of authenticity. Careful attention to detail in the reproduction of the ground colour of the wallpaper, and particularly the use of wool rather than synthetic flock, combined with toning by hand *in situ* after hanging, have achieved a remarkably discreet juxtaposition between old and new. Those who knew the room well before the fire will recognise certain differences, but others would have to look very hard.

The principal change arises from the decision to conserve and patch surviving unfaded rectangles behind pictures and pier-glasses but not to reproduce them where they had been destroyed. Thus Uppark *cognoscenti* will notice that the line of carmine shapes in the lower register of the main (east) wall is no longer visible (having been revealed when the *c.*1820 picture-hang was altered in about 1970). Otherwise, the 1820 hang has been repeated where feasible, so there are still large areas of unfaded wallpaper behind the two large paintings by Giordano on the east wall and behind Sir Harry's portrait by Reynolds over the fireplace. None of this is noticeable unless it is pointed out, and the vindication of this approach is that the conserved wallpaper upholds the subtle harmony of other contents of the room, notably the carpet and curtains which have also undergone a similar ordeal by fire. Nevertheless, the *Guardian*, of 27 April 1995, branded the conservation of the Red Drawing Room wallpaper as 'deranged perfectionism'.

Equally 'deranged', and equally consistent with the overall philosophy of Uppark's repair, was the painstaking reproduction of other wallpapers. Only fragments of these had survived, and upstairs not even fragments, so there was no possibility of repeating the conservation approach pursued in the Red Drawing Room. In the Little Drawing Room, a crimson flock paper printed on a powdered mica ground had faded to a purply pink, and, as in the Red Drawing Room, the original colour was preserved behind the pictures. Fragments of faded and unfaded wallpaper survived the fire, and it was decided to copy the faded colour, which was more consistent with the patination of the contents of the room. The paper was probably the 'Satin Flock' hung in 1859 by Thomas Harland of Southwark. The curtains, though now also faded, are probably the 'mauve and crimson figured striped Merino damask' supplied in 1852 by the London upholsterer Charles Hindley of Oxford Street. Originally, the combination of curtains and wallpaper must have been rather striking – as in the Red Drawing Room, the new wallpaper probably replaced an earlier crimson flock of a more restrained type. Apart from the unusual ground (the addition of mica made it glossy), the post-fire manufacture of this wallpaper involved the same procedures as those in the Red Drawing Room paper and was made by the same firm.

In the Tapestry Bedroom, by contrast, the original paper (of which fragments were once again retrieved) had not been block-printed, but machine-made by running the paper through two metal and felt rollers transferring the pattern. The mid-nineteenth-century paper was probably hung by Sir Harry's widow. It is of lower quality than the block-printed papers of this date, being printed on a wood-pulp rather than a rag paper. Originally two shades of crimson, but faded to a coffee colour, the paper was hung as a border to the early eighteenth-century Brussels tapestries which

The original wallpaper in the Yellow Bedroom was made in France, *c.*1850. It incorporated seventeen colours, each requiring a separate wooden block. Robert Weston copied an identical paper surviving in a Parisian museum, reproducing the new paper by screen printing thirteen times.

were nailed to the wall with brass-headed upholstery nails. This curious combination of wallpaper and tapestry is also found at Petworth, and seems to have been a mid- to late nineteenth-century fashion. As the cost of reproducing the paper by the original metal roller method would have been prohibitive, screen-printing was adopted as the closest comparable technique. Robert Weston of Hamilton Weston Wallpapers Ltd, in London, copied the pattern by hand, giving attention to the original printing irregularities and to the effects of ageing. Thus, although the original was printed in two colours on grounded paper, the reproduction involved five screen-printings to copy convincingly the variation of colour caused by fading.

Upstairs in the private apartment, few fragments of the set of block- and roller-printed wallpapers survived the fire; with one exception, these had to be reconstructed on the basis of photographs and other evidence. On this floor, some cost concessions had to be made in order to concentrate resources upon the principal state-rooms downstairs. Thus, the magnificent French Yellow Bedroom paper of *c.*1850–5 could not be block-printed, as originally, in seventeen colours. Despite this, Robert Weston achieved a superb reproduction by screen-printing thirteen times on to a traditional soft grey, hand-troughed matt ground. An incomplete pattern repeat, in identical colours, was traced to the Bibliothèque Fornay, in Paris, and served as a model for the reproduction of what was, at the time, one of the most extravagant wallpapers available in France.

Hamilton Weston Ltd's screen-printing also convincingly reproduced the English dove-grey and lilac embossed wallpaper of *c.*1850 or a little later in a first-floor bedroom hung with tapestry before the fire. A fragment of original paper was found in the collection of Uppark wallpaper given to the Victoria & Albert Museum in 1969 by Mrs Richard Meade-Fetherston-haugh. Here are numerous samples obtained by Sir Harry's widow in the course of her usually discreet but occasionally colourful modernisation of Uppark. The embossed relief effect of the upstairs Tapestry Bedroom paper was achieved in *trompe-l'oeil* by additional shadow and highlight screens. Another paper copied by Robert Weston by reference to the Victoria & Albert Museum collection, was the late nineteenth-century English roller-printed paper of leaves on a diapered ground in the bedroom adjoining the Print Room.

More complicated, because it had to be reconstructed almost entirely from photographs, was the manufacture of the mauve, white and gold bordered paper in the family dining-room, originally the dressing-room of the two principal châtelaines of Uppark: Sarah Lethieullier and Mary Ann Bullock. The ground was originally roller-printed; the border block-printed. Both were reproduced by Robert Weston using screen-printing, a process made possible by the fortunate discovery, in a shoe-box full of family photographs, of a fragment of the original paper with a gilt fillet in *trompe-l'oeil.*

Next door, in what was the lady of Uppark's bedroom but which had become a drawing-room by the time of the fire, the walls were hung with an eighteenth-century turquoise-blue flock wallpaper, probably put up by Sir Matthew. A bill was presented in 1831 for supplying and hanging 'Damask Flocked Paper Light Blue – Blue ground', but this may have been for the adjoining dressing-room. In 1931, Lady Meade-Fetherstonhaugh found this paper 'burnt by the sun and light'. In 'the N.E. Chamber Room' she found 'a trunk case containing rolls of flock paper previously left over from papering the walls when Sir Matthew redecorated the house in 1745 [sic]. These papers are all stamped with the George II Royalty Stamp, and I have been told that there existed at Liss [a village five miles away] a well known wallpaper Industry, so it is possible that Sir Matthew procured the flock wallpapers of Uppark locally.' The papers could well have been made at Liss, and although the leftovers that Lady Meade-Fetherstonhaugh put 'aside for Museum interest' did not survive the fire (a fragment of a different

A photograph taken in 1978 of the Family Drawing Room on the first floor, and showing the eighteenth-century flock paper repaired by Lady Meade-Fetherstonhaugh in 1931. This room was totally destroyed in the fire.

eighteenth-century flock was given to the Victoria & Albert Museum in 1969), it is possible that the original eighteenth-century Red Drawing Room crimson flock discovered after the fire was a product of the Liss manufactory.

With 'a few paper rolls' of the Blue Bedroom paper (an extraordinary survival from the mid-eighteenth century, and indicative of Sir Matthew's foresight), Lady Meade-Fetherstonhaugh 'set to work to repaper portions of the walls' where the damage was most obvious. Her method was similar to the procedure followed in the Red Drawing Room after the fire. First, she overlaid the most damaged sections with new paper; then she 'painted over faded portions of the paper to harmonise between the more faded pieces and the pieces we had renewed.' From the shadows of an old picture-hang, she deduced that the Neapolitan views by Ruiz (now in the Red Drawing Room) were originally hung here and restored them to the room. Her diary entry for 14 December 1931 records her satisfaction:

Moved into Blue Bedroom and slept there with Jim [the Admiral's nickname]. Bliss in the beauty of it. Greens and blues – white and gold mirrors – firelight and flowers. I remember I lay in bed and felt thrilled with its beauty and charm. Note: I feel certain that I shall one day find that this was Sarah Lethullier's [sic] room.

Sadly, this magical interior is no more and not a fragment of the wallpaper survived, although it has now been replaced by a faithful copy based on old

The Print Room, *c.*1770, retains its original decor because the engravings and their backing paper were in course of conservation at the time of the fire. The prints were returned to their original positions after de-acidification and repair, by Allyson McDermott.

photographs and memories of its extraordinary marine blue-green colour. The new paper was devised by Tom Helme and block-printed by Dennis Savage at Silvergate Papers, in Norfolk. Also destroyed in the flames were the parcel-gilt rococo chimneypiece with its chinoiserie overmantel, the fixed oval pier-glasses suspended by ribbons of painted wood, the pictures (including a portrait by Batoni) and a superb pair of English eighteenth-century commodes veneered with Chinese lacquer.

The tally of destruction on the first floor is only mitigated by the survival of the Print Room whose engravings, mounted on paper painted a straw colour, were in Orde Solomon's London conservation studio at the time of the fire. They were removed, in advance of the building repairs that caused the burning of Uppark, both for safety (some structural work was required uncomfortably close by) and to arrest their obvious deterioration. Unfortunately, a carved and painted mirror of *c.*1770, and integral to the original scheme, was destroyed, having been packed up in a box and stored here when the room was dismantled.

The practice of sticking engravings to a papered wall within paper 'frames' and 'hung' from paper ribbons to create a paper picture gallery seems to have originated in England, whence it spread to the Continent. In 1753, Horace Walpole described his Print Room at Strawberry Hill as 'hung with yellow paper and prints in a new manner invented by Lord Cardigan [the 4th Earl, 1712–90], that is with black and white borders printed'. In theory, at least, such rooms could be created by amateurs but, as today, professionals were often hired to execute them. In 1762, Thomas Chippendale fitted up a dressing-room at The Hatch, Ashford, in Kent, by lining and colouring the walls and 'Cutting out the Prints, Borders and Ornaments and hanging them in the Room Complete'. It was possible to buy borders, ribbons and other decorative elements from engravers and print-sellers who made or supplied them for the purpose.

One such maker was Francis Vivarès (1709–80), part of whose stock-in-trade survives at the Victoria & Albert Museum, and who may well have been involved at Uppark judging by the fact that in 1774 Sir Matthew paid £5 15s to 'Mrs. Vivaro for Prints'. The prints are mainly after Italian, Flemish and Spanish Old Masters, including a series of engravings depicting scenes of witchcraft and alchemy after David Teniers the Younger (1610–90). The only contemporary print (and indeed the only English one) is Fisher's engraving (1762) of Sir Joshua Reynolds's painting *Garrick between Tragedy and Comedy*, at Waddesdon Manor, in Buckinghamshire. The room must therefore be later than 1762, and, given that it is a consequence of Sir Matthew's remodelling of the Saloon beneath, it must have been constructed in about 1770.

Tradition has it that Lady (Sarah) Fetherstonhaugh was responsible for the Print Room's arrangement. Her skill as an amateur artist makes this very likely. She may also have painted the individual flowerpots and flowers beneath the dado, although they seem somewhat coarse compared with Lady Fetherstonhaugh's signed watercolours and may have been added later, possibly in the 1840s. The tiered and symmetrical arrangement of the prints is well balanced, indicating a degree of forethought that is always apparent in the best surviving print rooms. These are rare, as is the un-touched state of the Uppark room, whose appearance has been carefully preserved in its conservation.

Print rooms were often created in dressing-rooms, and even though the original function of this room is unknown, it was certainly used as such by Admiral Meade-Fetherstonhaugh from 1931. A telescope stood in the window so that he could scan the distant Solent and amuse himself by commenting upon his colleagues' seamanship. He, or his predecessors, must also have had a wash-stand, judging by the copious water damage in the centre of the west wall, where the shadow of the destroyed mirror is still evident. Paper conservation preserved such evidence of human occupation, the brief being to undertake the minimum of restoration, consistent with the well-being of the prints and their support, rather than seeking to redress the wear and tear of over 200 years. As the Print Room was the sole surviving element of a beautifully shabby set of rooms, such sensitive and accurate treatment was vital.

Allyson McDermott's examination of the paper to which the prints were attached revealed that small sheets of mould-made rag paper, with occasional mixed fibres of rag or hemp, were first stuck to the walls as a lining paper (paper was not manufactured in rolls until about 1835). To this surface, additional paper sheets were then applied with a mixture of starch and animal glue. The whole was then painted with straw-yellow paint – the usual, but not the sole, background colour for print rooms. This is an excellent foil for the monochrome engravings, now discoloured to brown as a result of the acidity of the paper and glue. The printed borders are of two types and widths: narrow to simulate wooden wallpaper fillet and used, for the same purpose, to hide the metal tacks which supported the paper wall lining; and broad at dado level to simulate a dado rail.

The engravings and flowerpots were separated from the lining paper as the first stage of conservation. The lining paper had been considerably degraded by water, mould and insect attack. In places it had come away from the wall, or was split and abraded. Continual attempts at improvement had involved wholesale repainting or retouching. Analysis revealed that the several layers of overpaint could be removed to reveal the original well-bonded paint surface. The yellow painted paper was separated from the rag lining paper by controlled rinsing in water, which also reduced its acidity and that of the old and potentially harmful glue. Afterwards, not only was much of the overpaint and residual staining removed, but also the strength and texture of both layers of original paper were greatly improved.

Conserving the prints was more complicated due to the imbalance between the thick paper of the engravings and the thinner paper of their 'frames' which had caused distortion and splitting. The engravings were lightly de-acidified with cold water from the back in order not to affect the heavily inked surfaces. The borders, bows and plant-pots were immersed in water and damage was treated locally as it would have been impossible to have trimmed a lining paper around all the delicately cut-out decorations. Some obviously unsightly gaps in the borders, where the original paper had disappeared completely, were filled in, the new paper being engraved in carbon ink from copper plates as originally. For this, Lindsay Farrimond worked on an intaglio press at Thomas Bewick's Northumbrian birthplace at Cherryburn (another National Trust property). Small losses and damages in the borders and frames were left alone. Similarly, only local retouching was done so as to preserve the feeling of a room that had not previously undergone any treatment.

A dramatic footnote to this account of the conservation of Uppark's wallpapers was provided by the discovery in the Little Parlour, beneath several subsequent layers, of a section of hand-painted eighteenth-century Chinese wallpaper depicting, with great delicacy, birds roosting among flowering branches. This wallpaper would most probably have formed the setting for Sir Matthew's collection of furniture inlaid with Chinese lacquer. The most exotic piece, a cabinet set not only with lacquer but also with Italian *pietra dura* panels and Neo-classical ivories, still stands in the Little Parlour.

Left: The Little Parlour as restored after the fire, in accordance with evidence through paint analysis of its early nineteenth-century decoration.

Above: After the fire, mid eighteenth-century painted Chinese wallpaper was discovered during examination of salvaged wallcoverings from the Little Parlour (*left*). It must have been put up *c.*1750 by Sir Matthew to provide a setting for his *chinoiserie* furniture and later papered over. Strikingly similar paper is hung in the Chinese Bedroom at Felbrigg Hall, Norfolk (*right*). It was supplied during Paine's alterations in 1752.

It is comparable to designs published by Chippendale in 1754 and by Mayhew & Ince in 1762, although its maker is not documented. The room was given its present Neo-classical overlay by Sir Matthew himself in *c.*1770, and it is possible that its original chimneypiece (now destroyed) was the exuberantly carved chinoiserie/rococo wooden surround and overmantel which stood in the blue-papered drawing-room above the Little Parlour before the fire. The great period for the importation of Chinese papers into Europe was between 1740 and 1790. It is interesting to note, in view of James Paine's probable involvement at Uppark, that similar Chinese paper was hung, with his advice, at Felbrigg in 1752, having been acquired through the East India Company in the previous year.

7: The Conservation of the Contents

THE HISTORY OF THE UPPARK COLLECTION effectively begins in 1747, when Sir Matthew Fetherstonhaugh set about the decorating and furnishing of his new country seat. His varied interests, ranging from the arts and sciences via politics and farming, were broadened by his marriage in 1746 to Sarah Lethieullier, from a family of rich and cultivated Huguenot bankers. Her cousin, Smart Lethieullier, FRS, FSA, was a prominent antiquary and collector. Sarah is thought to have brought to Uppark the canopy and hangings of the Prince Regent's Bed as well as the famous dolls'-house, whose façade bears the Lethieullier arms. She was a competent amateur artist, whose watercolour drawings of flora and fauna hang in the Red Drawing Room. The set of four marine landscapes by Joseph Vernet (1714–89), illustrating the *Four Times of Day*, and two river landscapes were commissioned by Sarah's brother Benjamin (like his father, a director of the Bank of England) in 1751. However, Sir Matthew himself acquired the majority of the Old Master pictures and inherited a group of family portraits.

Sir Matthew's purchase of Uppark, and his elevation to the baronetcy, followed the bequest of £400,000 from a kinsman, Sir Henry Fetherstonhaugh (1654–1746). This enormous legacy enabled Sir Matthew to indulge both his taste for building and his inclination to travel. With major alterations at Uppark already in train, he and his wife, accompanied by a family retinue, made a leisurely progress through France to Italy, where sojourns in Venice, Florence, Rome and Naples laid the foundations of the Uppark collection. Sir Matthew liked buying pictures in sets, presumably with an eye for their decorative effect. In Venice, he acquired eight views of the city from Canaletto's studio; in Rome, no less than nine portraits and two subject pictures were commissioned by the Fetherstonhaugh party from Pompeo Batoni (1708–87), soon to become the most fashionable painter in the city; in Naples, as well as four Neapolitan landscapes by the obscure view-painter Tommaso Ruiz (active in the 1740s), Sir Matthew may also have purchased the *Prodigal Son* series of five paintings by Luca Giordano (1632–1705). In Italy Sir Matthew also acquired the pair of scagliola table slabs which were buried under ash and debris in the Stone Hall on the night of the fire.

The chandelier from the Red Drawing Room had to be painstakingly restored. Here, drawn glass is being ground by Conor Brennan to produce one of the bevelled arms (see also pp. 161 and 162).

Sarah Lethieullier,
wife of Sir Matthew
Fetherstonhaugh,
painted by Pompeo
Batoni in 1751 in Rome
during their Grand Tour.
This is the pendant to
Batoni's portrait of
Sir Matthew, (p.55).

An earlier Continental tour in 1748 (to Spa in Belgium, in an attempt to improve Sir Matthew's poor health) may explain the presence at Uppark of Flemish tapestries and certain Flemish pictures in the Dining Room and the Red Drawing Room. Equally, these and other pictures whose provenance is unclear could have been acquired at auction or from dealers in England. Certainly, as a generalisation, most of the good pictures at

John Boultbee's painting of Sir Matthew's race-horses, *Prophet and Surprise*, in course of conservation. Helen White is removing the varnish blanched by firewater.

Uppark derive from Sir Matthew's activities as patron and collector. In 1753, he observed: 'I have acquir'd Reputation by my Purchases in Italy those Pictures particularly I bought at Naples are much esteem'd.' His best pictures – the Italian and Flemish landscapes and subject pictures in particular – were probably purchased for his London house. This would explain Horace Walpole's observation in 1770 that at Uppark there were 'no tolerable pictures but five or six of Sir Matthew, his Wife, and their relations by Pomeio [sic] Batoni'. If Uppark only contained family portraits this would have been typical of contemporary practice to concentrate important pictures and sculpture in the capital – the 1764 inventory of Petworth, for example, lists portraits alone and the cream of the 2nd Earl of Egremont's much finer collection then hung in Egremont House, in Piccadilly. Fortunately, due to the speed of their rescue from the flames and their emergency conservation throughout the night of the fire, the Uppark pictures only needed studio repair on a comparatively minor scale. The Trust, however, took the opportunity to clean and restore the more important paintings, such as those by Giordano and Batoni.

Sir Harry Fetherstonhaugh inherited his father's interest in the arts, but his youthful extravagance put paid to any building schemes, at least until his late middle age. He was forced to retrench by the sale of the Whitehall house in 1787 for 12,000 guineas (it had cost just over £10,000 to build) and this probably occasioned the transfer of pictures and furniture to Uppark. Sir Harry's charm and easy manner (evident in Batoni's portrait painted on the Grand Tour in 1776) commended him to the Prince of

Wales (later George IV), who said of Uppark that 'Newmarket Races were dull in comparison'. From at least 1784 until about 1810, when a quarrel excluded Harry from the Prince's inner circle, the pair were close friends. Harry was not only valued as a connoisseur of horses and women, but also advised the Prince on more serious aesthetic questions.

Sir Harry's forte was his discriminating taste for the French decorative arts, an enthusiasm shared by the Prince and his companions. Although some of the finest pieces (including Louis XVI furniture by Martin Carlin and J.H. Riesener) were sold in 1911, the Uppark collection is still notable for its French eighteenth- and early nineteenth-century furniture, porcelain and fittings, many acquired by Sir Harry personally or through intermediaries in Paris. It was probably the Vestibule at the Prince's London palace, Carlton House, that inspired Sir Harry's one considerable interior alteration at Uppark. Repton's Dining Room likewise incorporates busts of notable Whigs (Sir Harry, like his father, was a long-serving but taciturn MP), which gave *gravitas* to the scene that in 1780 or 1781 had reputedly witnessed the Bacchic spectacle of Sir Harry's mistress, later Emma Hamilton, dancing naked on the mahogany table. In 1825, Sir Harry's former predilection for nubile girls of a lower social class resurfaced dramatically in his proposal of marriage to Mary Anne Bullock, fifty years his junior. Despite society disapproval ('I hear Sir Harry Fetherston is to marry his Cook,' exclaimed the Duke of Wellington's confidante) the marriage lasted happily until Sir Harry's death in 1847.

Mary Ann, who had been packed off to Paris to acquire the social graces, seems to have been a sensible and charitable woman, who, together with her younger sister Frances, apparently devoted her life to the preservation of Uppark as 'Sir 'Arry 'ad it'. However, the tradition that Uppark was preserved as a shrine is exaggerated. Wallpapers were papered over afresh, rooms were redecorated, curtains and carpets acquired, the central heating system extended.

More to the point in this context, the Uppark collection ceased to grow with Sir Harry's death; indeed the only changes were to be the depletions of 1911 and the 1970s. The inventory of 1874, drawn up on Mary Ann's death, is the first to survive since 1724 and describes the contents in detail from attic to basement. The earliest photographs reveal that these crowded typically Victorian arrangements remained largely static until a certain amount of reshuffling in the 1930s. The pictures, however, remained in the same positions from at least *c.*1820, the date of a series of picture-hanging diagrams, until changes had to be made following the transfer of certain pictures into the upstairs private apartment in about 1970.

The petrification of Uppark after Sir Harry's death is most graphically illustrated by the preservation of his white and gold décor in the Saloon and Dining Room and by the remarkable fact that the picture-hang in both rooms has remained unaltered, so that the shadows on the paintwork reflect

The Dining Room,
remodelled by Repton
between 1812 and 1814.
Even after the fire, the
room retains much of his
white and gold decoration
and the contents were
returned to their former
positions.

the positions recorded in the diagrams. The decorative brass picture hooks
also remain in place, the pictures being suspended in several rooms by
silken ropes (dyed crimson or yellow to match the curtains) from picture
rails or from hooks fixed at cornice level. The original ropes had disappeared by the 1970s, but have been replaced since the fire on the basis
of old photographs and by reference to the similar chandelier cords.

The Uppark tradition of guardianship was heroically upheld by Lady
Meade-Fetherstonhaugh, whose husband inherited in 1930. She devoted
her life to the stewardship of Uppark and in particular to the preservation
of its historic textiles. The silk damask festoon curtains, which she thought
to be Italian of c.1740, were hanging in tatters. With the advice of Miss
Symonds of the Royal School of Needlework, she and her assistants set
about a decade of systematic conservation, which involved lifting the dirt
in an infusion of the plant *Saponaria officinalis*, then laying down the fluffy
damaged silk and sewing it in place at the loom. Once rehung, the curtains
were resprayed biannually with *Saponaria* and spring water.

Every element of the collection was inspected and repaired. Pictures and
furniture were rescued from attics, and the romantic history of Uppark

and its owners emerged from the often 'rat-eaten' documents that she brought to light. Her love of Uppark and its collection is evident on every page of her book *Uppark and its People* (written with the naval historian Oliver Warner), and in her diary and other writings. While she would have been devastated by the fire, she would surely have rallied quickly and set to work. She would certainly have been intrigued by the expertise which was brought to bear on the damaged contents, and perhaps gratified that her approach to conservation was once again the guiding principle and inspiration behind five years of careful and thorough repairs.

Decisions about the conservation of damaged contents were taken by the contents committee, the counterpart of the design team supervising the building repairs. It was chaired by Peter Pearce and included Nigel Seeley, who advised on all conservation issues, Anna Bennett, a freelance archaeological conservator responsible for co-ordinating the tendering process, the subsequent repairs and the reinstallation of the contents into the house, and Kevin Whitehead, who ensured that budgets were not exceeded and that value for money was obtained. Christopher Rowell, also a member of the committee, specified the work in advance and inspected it in progress to ensure that no one object looked out of kilter with its neighbours or with the faded decoration of the rooms preserved after the fire.

As with the building, the work was split into 'packages', which were put out to tender. Financial control was paramount, not only in relation to the Trust's insurers, but in view of the Trust's legal action against Haden Young Ltd, whose subcontracted leadworkers had perpetrated the fire. Every element of expenditure might therefore have to be justified in a court of law. In insurance terms, there was an important distinction between the building and its contents. Whereas the building was insured for the full value of its restoration, the contents were insured for a maximum of £400,000 in respect of repairable damage only, as in the case of all the Trust's houses. This reflects not only the inordinate cost of insuring one of the world's largest and most valuable art collections, but also the pragmatic principle that a destroyed Rembrandt is, quite literally, irreplaceable. Thus, in pursuing its successful claim against Haden Young Ltd, the Trust sought (and obtained) full compensation for its uninsured loss of approximately £1 million in respect of Uppark's contents.

Without Lady Meade-Fetherstonhaugh's campaign of textile conservation, there is no doubt that Uppark's reputation as a house remarkably unaltered since the eighteenth century would not have persisted to quite the same extent. Whatever the date or origin of the silk damask festoon curtains (whether eighteenth- or early nineteenth-century, whether Italian, French or English), their survival *in situ* in the 1930s was remarkable enough for Lady Meade-Fetherstonhaugh to make their preservation, and that of the associated Uppark textiles, something of a personal crusade. Apart from the Victoria & Albert Museum's repair with adhesives of the

Prince Regent's bedspread in about 1970, the Trust subsequently followed Lady Meade-Fetherstonhaugh's lead in textile conservation. Silk that was beginning to lift was carefully laid down and sewn into place or 'couched', with silk in parallel couching lines; as a less radical alternative, it might be kept in place by dyed silk net laid over curtains, or over the upholstery of bed or seat furniture. The fire brought forward, and made more complicated, what could in due course have been a major course of treatment to arrest fifty years of light damage and wear since Lady Meade-Fetherstonhaugh's initial repairs. After the fire, and emergency conservation, the textiles were carefully packed up to await subsequent studio repair.

Given the extent of the fire damage, the decision could well have been taken to unpick Lady Meade-Fetherstonhaugh's work and replace silk couching 'tramlines' with finer modern silk, in effect making the twentieth-century restorations less visible. Instead, her couching has been preserved and imitated where broken by fire damage: for example, one of the Red Drawing Room curtains was torn in half in the urgent endeavour to rescue it, and replacement couching lines, in silk of equal thickness, now fills the gap, thus disguising the join. Even her cotton linings have been preserved where possible. Her practice was to use the original woollen tammy lining as a support for the frayed damask. After cleaning, the damask would be sewn on to the lining with couching thread running in long parallel lines.

Above: Lady Meade-Fetherstonhaugh and her assistants working at the loom in the Saloon in the mid-1950s.

Left: Upholstery on an embroidery frame in 1955, in the course of repair, showing Lady Meade-Fetherstonhaugh's distinctive 'couching', or laying down of frayed silk with parallel stitches of thread.

The original lining would then disappear beneath a new cotton lining dyed to match.

After the fire, Guy Evans, a London silk merchant who specialises in the accurate copying of historic silks, acted as the Trust's consultant on the procurement of new silk and *passementerie* (trimmings). Five curtains had to be completely replaced with new silk hand-woven in Lyons by Maison Prelle; the fringing was made in Paris by La Passementerie Nouvelle, with new tammy linings and silk tapes supplied by Anna and Neil Warburton of Context Weavers, in Lancashire, and all were hand-sewn together in Old Windsor, Berkshire, by Eileen Reay, an expert seamstress, after close scrutiny of the original method of construction. The copying of the faded colours allowed the new curtains to blend in (more happily than was expected) with their older, somewhat ravaged, neighbours. The *passementerie*, with hand-knotted fringe where appropriate, was coloured *en suite*, no attempt being made to imitate the blackening by age of the pendant corkscrew torsades that punctuate the fringes.

In two instances – in the Red Drawing Room and the Saloon – the bottom half of curtains that had burnt at the top and dropped to the floor could be reused. Here, it was much more doubtful whether the new silk, following the irregular contour of the repaired fragment, would be successfully disguised. The folds, created when a festoon curtain is drawn up, provide useful camouflage. The results have been remarkably congruous, although the new pale yellow silk in the Saloon had to be toned down by an overlay of a transparent polyester called 'Stabiltex'. Thus, as much as possible of the original stuff was repaired and replaced *in situ*. The remnants were preserved for long-term storage, together with a red silk curtain from the Little Parlour, placed in store by Lady Meade-Fetherstonhaugh in accordance with her admirable practice of leaving one item in each set unrestored as a record of its original state. This Little Parlour curtain is therefore an extremely rare survival of a curtain which may have been made up in the eighteenth century.

Three conservation studios won the tenders for the repair of the curtains. The Trust's own Blickling Textile Conservation Workroom, in Norfolk, took on the five yellow curtains from the Saloon which are probably early nineteenth-century. The Textile Conservation Studio at Hampton Court repaired the plain yellow satin curtains from Repton's Dining Room and the mid-Victorian wool and silk curtains from the Little Drawing Room. All the surviving red silk curtains (from the Little Parlour and the Red Drawing Room) were conserved by the Textile Conservation Centre, also at Hampton Court. To reduce intervention to a minimum, most of the curtains did not need to be washed before conservation. Their dousing with fire-hoses, natural drying and surface-cleaning after the fire had in fact improved their appearance and reduced their acidity to an acceptable level. Only the Dining Room curtains were washed (in special tanks

Above: Conservators from the Hampton Court Textile Conservation Centre rehanging the Red Drawing Room curtains.

Below: Photographs from a family album compiled in the early 1930s, showing (*left*) a Little Parlour curtain in tatters; and (*right*) the curtain after Lady Meade-Fetherstonhaugh had repaired it.

The ground floor Tapestry Bedroom in 1970, showing the family-owned early eighteenth-century Brussels tapestries subsequently sold to the American National Bank & Trust Company of Chicago. Since the fire, the Bank has returned the tapestries to Uppark, having accepted a replacement set donated anonymously by a benefactor of the National Trust.

at Hampton Court). Luckily, this necessary measure did not unduly alter the faded appearance of the curtains – an essential element of the Dining Room's patination, even after the fire. When rehung, all the curtains were fixed to the pelmets by Velcro (rather than by nails as before) so that they could be removed more easily in case of emergency or for maintenance.

Other decorative textiles at Uppark included a set of elaborate tasselled bell-pulls, several of which were destroyed. After conservation and netting (of the ropes as well as the tassels), they were replaced *in situ* (the bell-pull system, installed *c.*1800 and renovated in 1836, no longer worked before the fire and remains inoperative, but the fittings – bells, wires and bell-boards – were put back after repair). Even more elaborate are the double-tasselled crimson chandelier cords in the Little Parlour and Red Drawing Room. Probably supplied in 1836 by Edward Bailey of Mount Street, in London, a firm patronised by George IV, they were already in a parlous state in 1933 when Lady Meade-Fetherstonhaugh found the wooden core of the tassels and pendant bobbles 'rotten with worms'. It is remarkable that even after the ceilings had fallen on them, the repair of these fragile tassels rendered them robust enough for open display. In the process, the silk of the tassels was teased back into place and netted by Caroline Pilkington of the Textile Conservation Centre. Only the hanging cords were renewed (originally silk, but replaced in 1932 with 'patent 109 towing line'

Above: One of the yellow damask curtains from the Saloon at the Trust's Textile Conservation Workroom at Blickling Hall, Norfolk (*left*). Emergency conservation, by Melanie Leach, to remove ash and debris from the silk upholstery of the state bed (*right*).

Left: Poppy Singer and Annabel Wylie conserving part of the Prince Regent's Bed in their studio.

by the Seaman Rigger of the Royal Yacht, and now again rewoven in silk over a metal core).

There were two other major projects, both in their different ways more problematic than either the curtains or the decorative textiles. The Uppark state bed, regularly requested by the Prince Regent and so given his name, had miraculously survived a night within the burning house (the bed-spread had been carried to safety). The next day it was hurriedly dismantled and removed shortly before the ceiling collapsed. After drying, it was surface-cleaned by careful brushing and micro-vacuuming – no further cleaning proved to be necessary, or indeed desirable. The decision was taken early on that conservation alone would be sufficient and that the bed should be allowed to show its scars; there would be no replacement of silk, even on the front centre of the canopy where the carved wooden frame, to which the silk was stuck, was partly revealed by loss of the silk covering.

The front of the canopy also displays black scorch marks – again, the decision to accept such blemishes avoided unnecessary agonising and restoration. Occasionally, in a particularly damaged area, a fragment of silk damask carefully put aside in the 1930s by Lady Meade-Fetherstonhaugh served to fill a gap over which the surviving threads of the bed damask were laid (as over a bald man's pate) and fixed in place. Such 'new' fragments were stuck to the wooden frame by rabbit's skin glue – the adhesive that would originally have been used.

The Prince Regent's Bed is a composite piece put together after about 1760, the earliest possible date of the mahogany corner posts. The canopy, tester cloth, headcloth and bedspread belonged to an earlier bed or beds. The giltwood putti at the corners of the canopy are of seventeenth-century Continental origin. Formerly upstairs in the Prince Regent's Bedroom, the bed was moved downstairs in about 1970 into what was Sir Harry's bedroom but which had become a drawing-room by the end of the nineteenth century. It is called the Tapestry Bedroom after the early eighteenth-century Brussels tapestries, which were returned to Uppark in 1990, having been sold by the Meade-Fetherstonhaugh family in 1972. Their re-purchase involved the philanthropy of an enlightened English donor, who provided the money anonymously, and the generous compliance of the American National Bank and Trust Company of Chicago in whose banking hall the Uppark tapestries had hung for fifteen years. Before rehanging, they were repaired by Fiona Hutton and Frances Lennard, in their studio at Banwell, near Bristol.

The Prince Regent's Bed had been extensively repaired by Lady Meade-Fetherstonhaugh and her atelier in 1931–2, when the headcloth, with its embroidered decoration of c.1720, received 'as many as 20 lines of couching to the inch'. Once again, Lady Meade-Fetherstonhaugh's work was preserved, or added to in the same style, the whole being netted as an additional safeguard. The repair of the bed took Poppy Singer and Annabel Wylie, partners in their own textile conservation practice in Suffolk, over a year to accomplish, and was one of the most complicated and painstaking tasks undertaken. Annabel, in particular, had already proved her perseverance by working, as director of the Trust's Knole workroom, on the seventeenth-century King's Bed at Knole, in Kent, for no less than nine years. The fact that many people can still smell the fire in the Tapestry Bedroom is proof of the extent of damage to the bed, now extremely difficult to detect in most places.

That the same can be said of the carpet in the Red Drawing Room is even more surprising: it had been buried in wet sludge and sections had been burnt away. Its emergency treatment and subsequent repair and restoration dramatically illustrate the skills of its conservators at Jonathan and Heather Tetley's Carpet Conservation Workshop, near Salisbury, in Wiltshire. Hand-knotted in Axminster in c.1800, the central field is identical to

Conservation of the Axminster carpet, *c.*1800, dug out of the ruins of the Red Drawing Room: (*above*) undergoing cleaning at the Carpet Conservation Workshop near Salisbury; (*below*) a conservator sewing handwoven replacement sections of carpet to the repaired original. The closest possible match was achieved by selectively re-knotting or unknotting the new woven sections, and by shaving the pile to simulate the wear of the old carpet.

carpets at Osterley Park, in Middlesex, and Woburn Abbey, in Bedfordshire, although the borders are different. The matching hearth rug, dropped in the Saloon in an abortive attempt at rescue, was so badly damaged that there was no alternative but to store it as a relic. The carpet owes its survival to its structural stability, unweakened by its ordeal. Usually with carpets of this date and construction, the flax weft thread between the knots breaks down, causing the knots and warps to disintegrate. Unusually, the Uppark carpet had no split or broken sections, even though the pile was worn down to the base of the knots and there were areas where the knots had disappeared altogether, revealing bare warps. The surface responded well to immersion in a cleaning tank filled with water and mild detergent. There are still areas of irreversible scorching, especially along the folds, caused by being thrown hastily over the Red Drawing Room piano in the urgent evacuation of the house. As with the Prince Regent's Bed, such unsightliness had to be accepted and became less obvious once the furniture of the Red Drawing Room had been brought back.

The major decision related to the method of filling the gaps in one corner of the carpet where sections had been burnt away. Peter Auckland of Hill & Co., in London, specialist carpet suppliers, arranged for the losses to be rewoven by hand in Hungary in emulation of the original technique. New wool, carefully matched to the original by the Carpet Conservation Workshop, was used, taking into account both the colour and the age of the damaged carpet. But when the new sections were juxtaposed with the old the generalised range of twenty-five colours failed to deceive the eye. So, the requisite degree of subtlety was achieved by selectively reknotting the new infills to the exact shade, by shaving the pile to resemble the wear of the old carpet and by unknotting to imitate the occasional bare patch where the pile had been worn away. Conservation also rectified local damage caused by the fire, notably the holes made by the legs of the piano when they were forced through both the carpet and the floor in the collapse of the Red Drawing Room ceiling.

After the fire, the large French ormolu chandelier of $c.1800$ could be seen amid the wreckage of the Saloon where it had fallen. Despite being half buried in the debris, its arms were only slightly bent and the elaborate metal suspension chain was hardly damaged. Emergency conservation to this and all other metal objects salvaged from the ruins was undertaken by Rupert Harris, the Trust's adviser on metalwork conservation. The Saloon ormolu chandelier was subsequently dismantled by Plowden & Smith of Wandsworth, in London, and although teasing the arms back to shape required considerable care, its condition was so good that it proved unnecessary even to regild areas where the gilding had been abraded or lost. As with other objects, the view was taken that the chandelier should display its scars, that restoration should be kept to a minimum and that such minor blemishes would not be visible when it was back in place.

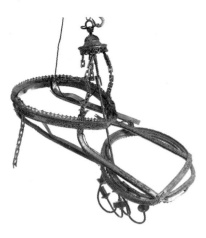

Conservation of the French ormolu lantern attributed to Pierre Gouthière, *c.*1785, from the Stone Hall: (*left*) as it emerged from the rubble; (*centre*) in course of conservation at Plowden & Smith's workshops in Wandsworth, London; (*right*) restored to the Stone Hall. Only a tiny proportion of its original ormolu decoration had to be replicated. The glass was copied to the exact profile from fragments retrieved.

By contrast, there was no sign after the fire of the two more delicate eighteenth-century lanterns in the Staircase Hall and Stone Hall. It was thought that if they had survived, they would clearly be severely damaged. These areas were not excavated for some considerable time after the fire, due to the dangerous condition of the surrounding masonry. Both lanterns eventually emerged from the rubble, completely flattened, but nevertheless largely intact. The careful sifting of the debris produced almost every minuscule piece of the gilded bronze ornament belonging to the Neoclassical French lantern in the Stone Hall and only a tiny section of frieze decoration and one small finial had to be copied. Also, sherds of glass provided evidence for the exact profile of the glazing and of the smoke cowl above, designed to protect the ceiling from soot. Comparison of the lanterns in their damaged and repaired states makes the point most vividly.

The Stone Hall lantern emerged with its original gilded bronze unblemished by the fire. This lantern of *c.*1785 is attributed to the Parisian maker Pierre Gouthière (*maître* 1758, *d.*1813), who made superlative

[149]

mounts for furniture and porcelain. Lanterns of this date and quality are extremely rare even in France, and a comparison can be made between the Uppark example and the lantern signed by Pierre-Philippe Thomire (1751–1843) in the Petit Trianon at Versailles, which was supplied to Queen Marie-Antoinette. It is possible that Sir Harry acquired this superb object (whose long and elegant chain allows a close view of its refinement) through the dealer Dominique Daguerre, from whom the Prince Regent made numerous acquisitions for Carlton House. The thought that this piece of museum quality, now seemingly in perfect condition, might have been thrown into a skip with the rest of the rubble, is a vindication of the thorough excavation after the fire.

The Staircase Hall lantern in Gothick style is English *c*.1760, and similar to a 'Lanthorn ... an hexagon in the Gothic Taste' published in Mayhew and Ince's *The Universal System of Household Furniture* (1762). Lanterns of an almost identical pattern hang in the portico of the State Apartments at Windsor Castle. In the course of repair, its original patinated bronze and gold decoration was revealed, where previously all was uniformly black with dirt. Only one gilt finial had to be replaced and the elaborate suspension chain survived intact. The glass was broken, but fragments allowed the plates to be recreated to the exact profile. The replacement eighteenth-century smoke cowl is from Chevening, in Kent. Bought in the sale there in 1993, it exactly fits the original Gothick metal rim, while the glass is of almost identical proportions.

Rescued from the house were huge numbers of miscellaneous fittings: picture hooks, curtain cloakpins, door-locks, window catches, bells and equipment from the servants' bell system, numerous sad remnants of magnificent mounts for French porcelain, ormolu feet from a fine pair of English lacquer commodes, together with a host of more mundane objects of household utility from the private apartments upstairs. All these had to be laid out in sets to quantify the losses. It emerged that none of the original fittings from the principal rooms on the *piano nobile* needed to be replicated, and more or less the same applied to the bedrooms of the first floor. Nor did any of the fireplace metalwork need replacement: all the register grates, ranging from the mid-eighteenth to the late nineteenth centuries, on the ground and first floors survived the fire (the first-floor fireplaces being almost sole survivors of otherwise gutted rooms). Even on the attic floor, the survival rate was considerable. Also, most of the fenders, pokers and shovels – from the elaborate expensive quality of the state rooms to the workaday variety in the attic – were retrieved. After conservation of the priority items initially by Rupert Harris, then by Dorothea Restorations Ltd, of Bristol, and Richard Rogers of Plowden & Smith (the main problem was rust), all this material was stored in metal containers, dehumidified to keep the atmosphere dry, pending re-installation.

Rupert Harris, the Trust's Adviser on Metal Conservation, restoring one of the salvaged eighteenth-century locks. Although apparently irretrievably damaged, almost all the original locks were replaced on the internal doors. The repair of these hand-made mechanisms was far cheaper than making authentic copies.

Most of the furniture – including outstanding pieces such as the dolls'-house and the satinwood *bonheur du jour* or writing-table in the Little Parlour, probably made for Sarah Fetherstonhaugh by John Cobb (*c*.1715–78) – was retrieved from the ground floor without having suffered significant harm. Treatment was limited to the rectification of minor fire damage so that the shabby appearance of gilding, in particular, would not be altered post-fire. It would have upset the delicate visual balance of the collection had newly resplendent sofas, chairs and picture frames appeared beside frayed upholstery, stained and patinated wallpaper, paint, gilded plaster and woodwork.

Five pieces of furniture were destroyed, although elements of three of these survived and will be used as evidence for eventual reconstruction. The two of which not a wrack remains were a painted mirror of *c*.1770, incinerated within its packing case where it stood in the Print Room after the removal of the engravings for repair in London, and from the Staircase Hall one of a pair of rococo parcel-gilt side-tables, of which the second remains undamaged in the Dining Room Servery. It is probable that this huge table, with a massive marble top, originally stood with its pendant on either side of the north door in the Saloon, where Repton's bookcases were later placed. They were among Sir Matthew's earliest commissions of the late 1740s. The destroyed table had been painted black, by tradition for Sir Harry's lying-in-state. Its total destruction is indicative of the ferocity of the fire in the Staircase Hall. The floorboards beneath were also destroyed, so the ashes simply fell into the basement.

Several ornamental mirrors and pier-glasses were severely damaged, although in most cases piecing in of missing carving or beading, and toning of the new sections and the local damages, avoided wholesale regilding. Neil Trinder Furniture Conservation of Sheffield undertook these repairs. Only one pier-glass from the Little Drawing Room retained its original eighteenth-century glass. Almost all the other eighteenth- or nineteenth-century glass was destroyed, either by the heat of the fire or by being smashed in the desperate attempt to save these fixed and often heavy pieces of decorative furniture.

Uppark's series of mid-eighteenth-century pier-glasses (the Neo-classical ones added later by Sir Matthew or Sir Harry are much less distinguished) was of paramount importance. None could be attributed definitely (in the absence of documents), but all were close to published designs by makers such as Thomas Chippendale and Matthias Lock (c.1710–65). The three biggest and finest were still in the burning house six hours after the fire had started, their size and weight having precluded initial rescue. Mercifully, the Little Drawing Room pier-glass was removed intact and almost undamaged – even its gilded bells were retrieved. In Chinese taste, and still markedly rococo, it is closely comparable to a design published in c.1752 by Lock. Given its miraculous escape, it is undoubtedly the most important of Sir Matthew's magnificent pier-glasses to have survived in its original condition.

In the adjoining Red Drawing Room, where the fire was raging fiercely, the frame of one of the pair of pier-glasses on the west wall was already on fire when, under the protection of showers of water, the firemen manoeuvred it from the wall. Both pier-glasses, trailing smoke and flames and their already damaged glass smashed to reduce the weight, were tilted sideways and manhandled through the windows. Emergency conservation was undertaken on the spot by Peter Thuring, the Trust's principal adviser on the treatment of gilded furniture. The photographs show clearly the extent of the damage. Both glasses had lost elements of carving, their gessoed and gilded surfaces flayed by the heat and water-damaged. Worst of all, the bottom section of the left-hand pier-glass had been reduced to charcoal. Repair would involve skilled carving, considerable experience of conservation and a good eye for the overall finished effect. The commission was won by Carvers & Gilders of Wandsworth, in south London, one of whose

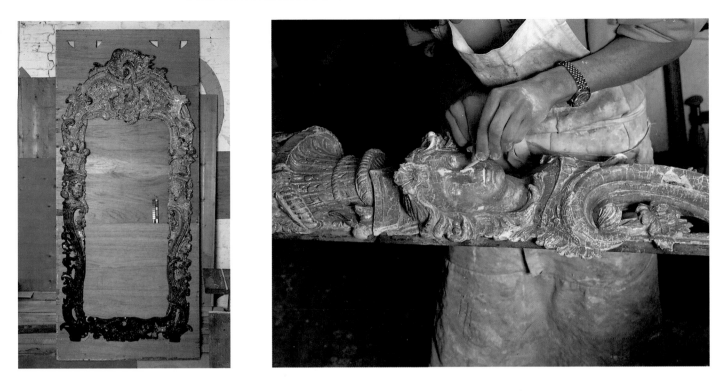

principal carvers is Christine Palmer. Analysis of the surfaces revealed that the overall water-gilding on gesso was probably not original, and that the mirrors had been painted stony white or parcel gilt (a combination of painting and gilding). The latter is more likely, both in view of the gilding elsewhere in the Red Drawing Room, for example the water-gilded wall-paper fillet, and because many pieces of furniture commissioned by Sir Matthew in the 1740s and 1750s are also parcel gilt.

The decision was taken, however, to remain loyal to the philosophy of returning to pre-fire appearance where practicable. Some of the gilding, which was probably nineteenth-century, survived – most completely where protected from the fire, for example, on the baskets of fruits and flowers upheld by male or female caryatids – and these areas were preserved and taken as a model for the tone of the new gilding. Sadly, in view of its irreversible damage, the base section of one frame had to be amputated. This was kept as an archival record, and may be seen in the Uppark exhibition.

Thanks to the patient work of Bob Taylor, one of Carvers & Gilders conservators, about 10 to 15 per cent of the damaged gilding was retained, even though the heat had cockled the surviving gold leaf so that it looked like cornflakes. The missing section was recarved by Christine Palmer, with recourse to the charred fragment and to extremely detailed photographs of the carving pre-fire. A full-scale drawing was made, the outline fretted

Conservation of one of the two pier glasses in the Red Drawing Room, attributed to Matthias Lock on the basis of an engraving of *c*.1744: (*left*) before conservation at Carvers & Gilders, Wandsworth, London. The charred base section had to be resected and recarved, while the destroyed glass was replaced with nineteenth-century glass acquired through the antiques trade; (*right*) a detail showing the extent of the damage.

[153]

Christine Palmer, of Carvers & Gilders, carving the new base of the more damaged Red Drawing Room pier-glass, to replace the irretrievably charred original section.

out and the form and detail refined during a month's carving work. The result is a *tour de force* of virtuoso carving, with a fluidity worthy of the original and all the more difficult to achieve due to the discipline of an exact copy. The Red Drawing Room rococo pier-glasses are attributed to Matthias Lock; the wild men and water-nymphs bearing baskets of fruit and flowers are similar to a design in his *Six Sconces* (1744). Their rescue and repair has restored two of the finest components of Sir Matthew's refurnishing of Uppark in the 1750s.

With one or two exceptions, notably the Little Drawing Room pier-glass, most of the pier-glasses had had their glass replaced in the nineteenth century. Despite protracted efforts, it proved impossible to commission modern mirror glass in accurate imitation of the ageing caused by disintegration of the original silvering (either tin or mercury or the slightly later metallic silver) with which the glass was coated. The only alternative was to compile, through the antiques trade, a stock of old glass which was then cut to size. Marilyn Smith, a freelance conservator, scoured the country for suitable pieces – sometimes acquired at a fraction of the cost that had been

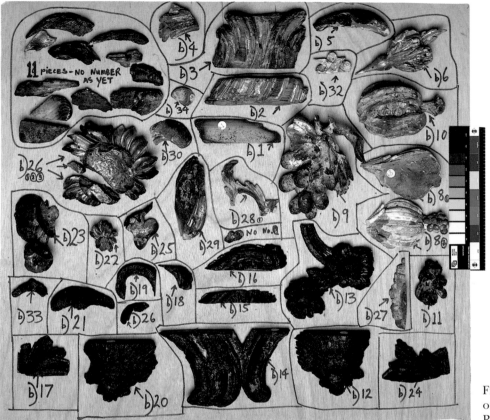

Fragments of frame from one of the Red Drawing Room pier-glasses.

Conservators at Carvers & Gilders turning the better preserved of the two Red Drawing Room pier-glasses during its repair.

estimated for specially manufactured modern glass. Most of this glass is nineteenth-century (eighteenth-century glass of a sufficient size could not be found – even then large plates were rare due to the difficulty of manufacture and to their great expense). Again, given the history of previous replacement of glass at Uppark, this was an authentic approach. The overall effect is now of a series of mirrors with glass that has apparently been within their frames for well over a century. The illusion of continuity remains consistent.

Perhaps the most difficult conundrum of all was presented by the pair of scagliola-topped side-tables in the Stone Hall. Trophies of Sir Matthew's Grand Tour and great rarities in themselves, they were better documented than any other element of his furniture collection. The extensive damage caused them by the fire is therefore particularly regrettable. Since they were overlooked in the first salvage, and impossible to rescue later, it is remarkable how much has survived – even of the wooden supports – and how great a revival of their former appearance has been achieved.

The slabs were commissioned, probably in 1750 when Sir Matthew and his relations are known to have been staying in Florence, from Don Petro Belloni (active 1740–60), who signed and dated one of them in 1754. Don Petro was assistant to Don Enrico Hugford (1697–1771), Abbot of the monastery of Vallombrosa near Florence, who was principally responsible for reforming the art of scagliola from 'being a cheap and easily worked substitute for marble and mosaic' into an art form valued for its own sake. Scagliola is a plaster made of pulverised selenite (gypsum) painted, fired and polished to resemble, in this case, *pietra dura* or inlaid marble. The Uppark tables are decorated with landscapes and decorative motifs, directly comparable in style to the products in *pietre dure* of the Grand Ducal Florentine workshops founded in 1588 by Ferdinand I de' Medici (1549–1609), Grand Duke of Tuscany. Undoubtedly, they were a cheaper alternative but scagliola of this date and origin is now far rarer than *pietra dura*. Indeed, apart from the Uppark pair, there are only five documented table-tops by Belloni (dated 1750 and 1756), all commissioned by Irish friends of Sir Matthew who were travelling in Italy at the same time.

Sir Matthew's introduction to Belloni probably came from the Abbot's brother, Ignazio Hugford, who was a half-Irish, half-Italian art dealer and Florentine *cicerone* to Grand Tourists. Belloni's clients had to be patient. Assuming that Sir Matthew's commission was given in 1750 at the earliest and that one slab is dated 1754, his tables may have taken up to five years. Sir Horace Mann, the British Resident in Florence, acted as intermediary. On 12 October 1753, Sir Matthew wrote to Mann: 'I hope you will excuse the Trouble of this, wch is to intreat the favr. of you to inquire of the Monk whether he has not done the two Tables I bespoke of him, & wch I beleive I mention'd to you when I left Florence.' An entry in Sir Matthew's account book for 27 March 1754 reads: 'For 2 tables at Florence on acct ... £25',

which implies that work was still in progress. The money was paid to Padre Belloni by Mann on the 29 March.

Once the scagliola tops were in England, the wooden supports were provided (this was normal practice to reduce the expense of transport from Italy). Originally gilded all over and now partially painted white, probably by Sir Harry in *c.*1815, the rococo consoles were probably made or supplied by John Bladwell (active 1724–68), the furniture-maker, upholsterer and upholder (supplier of furniture and furnishings), to whom Sir Matthew paid over £1,000 from 1747 onwards.

The tables had to be carefully excavated from the debris *in situ.* This delicate procedure was supervised by Fiona Allardyce, who also advised on the conservation of wall-paintings, and Trevor Proudfoot. Together with Sue Baumbach, both were involved in the subsequent studio repair of the tables, following the award of the tender to Cliveden Conservation Workshop. The left-hand table was found to be in the worse state. Only fragments of the wooden base survived, while the top was broken into eight pieces by the collapse of masonry. The scagliola layer had delaminated and shattered into over a hundred fragments. About 35 per cent of the decoration was destroyed, and much of the remainder irrevocably blackened. The other table fared much better. The top was broken in half, but most of the decorative detail survived in surprisingly good condition. The wooden support was also largely intact, despite the loss of half one leg and sections of the frieze.

Repairing the less damaged table involved the dowelling together with stainless steel of the two broken halves of the scagliola top, the filling of the central crack and its repainting in watercolour, the saturation of the whole surface with isinglass (fish glue) to consolidate the scagliola and the replacement of the destroyed sections of border with new scagliola made by Thomas Kennedy of the Cliveden Conservation Workshop. Finally, the

Conservation of one of a pair of scagliola-topped tables, early 1750s, from the Stone Hall: (*left*) Fiona Allardyce, then the Trust's Adviser on the Conservation of Wall Paintings, excavating the table after the fire: (*right*) the table in course of studio repair in the Cliveden Conservation Workshop. The join between the two halves of the broken scagliola has been disguised by infilling with plaster and painting in watercolour.

One of the scagliola table tops, photographed before the fire. It is signed and dated 1754 by the Florentine monk Don Petro Belloni, who took about five years to complete Sir Matthew's commission. In the course of the fire it was broken into eight pieces.

surface was saturated with cold-pressed linseed oil and when dry, given a coating of beeswax which was buffed to a shine appropriate to the age of the scagliola and its fire-damaged state. Originally, the clear shiny surface was built up by repeated applications of wax and the new owners were instructed to repeat the polishing at regular intervals. The restoration has been kept to a minimum, and the patchy appearance of more or less damaged sections simply has to be accepted.

The painting and gilding of the wooden support has been left entirely alone, except where local conservation was required or where new sections had to be toned in to match. This was done at Sheet, near Petersfield, by Hugh Routh and John Hartley, owners of the Tankerdale workshop and advisers on furniture conservation to the Trust. Both had taken part in the initial rescue of Uppark and the ensuing emergency conservation, and had also given valuable advice, with John Hart and Peter Thuring, on the conservation approach to the decorative carved woodwork. The carving of the missing elements of the scagliola table bases was a joint effort by the Tankerdale staff with the input of Ben Bacon and Alan Lamb, who

[158]

had also provided new carving for the decorative woodwork elsewhere in the house.

The particularly badly damaged pendant has undergone similar but much more laborious repair, beginning with the conservation and laying-out of the scagliola fragments so that the original design could be reconstructed in jigsaw fashion. Once the eight pieces of the broken slab were put back together and supported by stainless steel, the delaminated elements of the decorative surface were laid out again, revealing that the front half of the central landscape scene had been virtually obliterated. Despite this, the damaged scagliola was conserved rather than replaced. By contrast, the other half and much of the surrounding decoration was in good condition. Small losses were filled and the gaps in the pattern were repainted in water-colour toned to match the adjacent areas. After this, the missing edges were replaced in new scagliola and finally the whole surface was oiled and polished. The larger part of Bladwell's wooden console table has been recarved by Alan Lamb, who detected two hands in the original carving of this table and its pendant.

The other top, after initial emergency treatment. Although broken in half, most of the scagliola survived.

[159]

In about 1770, Sir Matthew bought two similar lead-glass chandeliers for the Little Parlour and the Red Drawing Room, the latter being slightly bigger. The Parlour had recently been given a Neo-classical ceiling, but the same style of chandelier was considered equally appropriate for the Drawing Room with its earlier rococo ceiling. Both have been tentatively attributed by Martin Mortimer, the senior director at Delomosne and Son Ltd, in Wiltshire, and a leading authority on glass chandeliers, to Christopher Haedy (active 1769–85), who had premises in London and Bath. In 1775, at Church Street, in Bath, Haedy advertised 'girandoles ornamented with festoons of entire paste, etc. etc.'. The small group of chandeliers attributed to him – which include a pair in the Library at Badminton, in Gloucestershire – are distinctive for the design of their solid stems and for their festoons of solid glass (paste) strung, as at Uppark, between notched spires. Haedy, an astute businessman and the son of a Bohemian glassmaker who came to London in the early 1720s, took over the celebrated firm of Maydwell & Windle, of 287 The Strand, in 1778. According to Mr Mortimer, 'the art of cutting reached one of few peaks at this time, a peak matched by the quality of the glass itself. The Uppark family of chandeliers . . . . are of a glass whose lead tint combines with brilliance of finish to produce a richness never surpassed . . . .'. The Uppark chandeliers were also notable before the fire for their unusually original condition, making their fate all the more unfortunate.

As at Hampton Court in 1986, where a late seventeenth-century crystal chandelier was retrieved and restored by Delomosne after burial in the wreckage of the palace, salvage trays were gradually filled, as excavation proceeded, with numerous pieces of cut glass. Some were crazed inside by the heat and cracked by subsequent dousing by fire-hoses; others were in pristine condition and suggestive of the jewelled hoard of some Indian potentate. As with all other categories of severely damaged objects, the surviving pieces were laid out. The first stage was the conservation of those elements of the chandeliers that could be reinstated. Broken spires and drops were conserved, and original pieces not in perfect condition replaced; the final judgement was postponed until the chandeliers could be reconstructed and rehung.

This preparatory work was undertaken at Thame, in Oxfordshire, by Sandy Davison. Missing spires and drops were obtained as antiques through the trade by Delomosne and Terry Brotheridge (who also put the chandeliers back together again), and the structural elements too damaged to repair were copied anew. This was made more challenging by the fact that modern glass, however expertly manufactured, has a lower lead content, and therefore reflects the light in a different way. Despite these initial reservations, the restoration of the chandeliers (the Little Parlour chandelier being more damaged than its companion) has proved an unqualified visual success. This is to the credit of Blue Crystal and Wilkinson's plc,

When they were repaired in 1933, Lady Meade-Fetherstonhaugh found these chandelier tassels, silk on a turned wooden core, 'rotten with worms'. It is remarkable that they survived within the rubble. This photograph shows them after initial treatment, and they have now been reinstated in the Red Drawing Room.

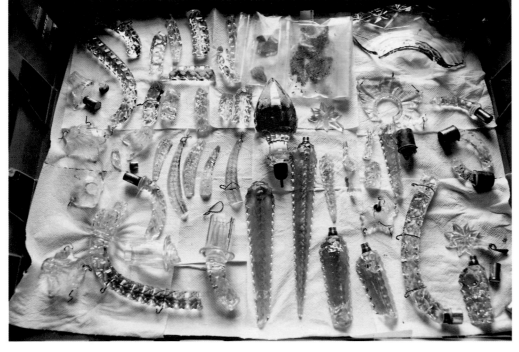

Salvaged fragments of the Red Drawing Room chandelier. After conservation, the better preserved elements were reincorporated in their original positions.

both of London, who shared the making and cutting of new arms, receiver bowls, canopies and other smaller constituents of the chandeliers that either had not survived or could not be reused. The proportion of original and partly original elements is approximately 70 per cent in the Red Drawing Room and 30 per cent in the Little Parlour. Now that the chandeliers are reunited with their crimson silk hanging tassels supplied in 1836, an expert eye is needed to discriminate between pre- and post-fire condition, although certain obviously damaged original pieces were reused in the cause of authenticity.

As the contents of Uppark gradually returned after conservation, they were initially stored at Petworth and then, after completion of the main building contract in June 1994, transported to the vacant woodworking shed on the east lawn. This was already air-conditioned, so that the new and conserved carving could be worked on in controlled conditions. Here, the furniture was marshalled before its reinstallation in the house, which had also been carefully monitored to ensure that the new environmental control systems were working properly. The return of the contents (in most cases to their old positions) had to be planned with military precision in a logical sequence. This was masterminded by Anna Bennett, with the advice of the Trust's Housekeeper Helen Lloyd and of the Southern Region's Conservator Madelaine Abey-Koch.

First, a thorough clean of the house cleared the dust raised by the builders and plasterers. The windows were also cleaned and coated with anti-ultraviolet-light film. In September 1994, the mirrors were rehung, followed by the pictures in October, and between January and February 1995 the curtains were refixed to the pelmets. The carpets were relaid by February, apart from the fragile Red Drawing Room carpet which was brought in at the last possible moment in April. The tapestries and the Prince Regent's Bed were returned in March.

The brunt of this taxing procedure was borne on a daily basis by Sophie Budden, a freelance gilding conservator who also undertook the final touches to the gilded woodwork, mirrors and picture frames, and Lisa Willis, Madelaine Abey-Koch's assistant, who helped to train the newly re-cruited cleaning staff. The conservators who had repaired objects – and who were therefore most familiar with the potential difficulties of rein-statement – were generally responsible for putting them back into the house and making the final adjustments on site. Almost all of Uppark's contents were home again a month before the opening of its doors in June 1995.

The Red Drawing Room chandelier after restoration. This is the larger of two chandeliers, early 1770s, attributed to Christopher Haedy who worked in London and Bath. The silk tassels were probably supplied in 1836 by Edward Bailey of Mount Street, London.

8: Epilogue

'UPPARK IS MORE THAN A HOUSE RESTORED. It is an argument won,' Simon Jenkins wrote in *The Times* of 3 June 1995. He went on to praise the repair and reconstruction of the building as 'a virtuoso monument to the British genius for craftsmanship'. Such comments confuted the view that the damaged house was incapable of repair and that there was no point in attempting what would only be at best a 'lifeless pastiche'. In the state rooms most of the contents have been restored to their original positions. The interior retains its old character and atmosphere, with the pale dry-scrubbed oak boards, the bright Downland light filtering into the rooms through half-drawn Holland blinds and the faded paintwork on the walls in the Saloon and the Dining Room. To those who knew it well before the fire, Uppark conveys a remarkable impression of being untouched by catastrophe.

Laurence Marks anticipated the reaction of many visitors in an article in the *Spectator* in May 1995, just before the house reopened: 'The result, astonishingly, is a triumph. To the non-specialist eye at least, most of the new work looks well wrought and a good match.' In particular, he described the freehand modelling of new plasterwork as 'crisp, bold and vivacious, faithful to the original yet never falling into dead pastiche'. Hugh Montgomery-Massingberd in the *Daily Telegraph* of 27 May 1995 felt that 'Nothing could better epitomise the purpose and point of the National Trust ... than this triumphant restoration.' He confessed that he set off 'fearing that I would find dear old Uppark, with its idiosyncratic combination of shabbiness and grandeur, all spick and span and sparkling new.' In *Building Design* of 5 May 1995, José Manser (married to the former President of the RIBA) also expressed her trepidation: 'Uppark with its dolls-house-like façade is looking magnificent, and the interiors have all the serene elegance I remember. Almost all the furniture in the ground-floor show rooms was saved, and that is back in place, frayed upholstery, faded drapes, worn surfaces and all. Don't expect (or dread) the shiny perfection of Harrods' furniture department, for you won't find it.' Joanna Watt, in *Perspectives in Architecture* of June 1995, was equally positive: 'The National Trust has recreated the interior and patina of the house with astounding accuracy. But it has done so under a hail of criticism.'

The restored Saloon, looking towards the Red Drawing Room. The decision to conserve Repton's white and gold decoration, *c.*1815, and to relay the dry scrubbed floorboards, has retained much of the room's previously untouched atmosphere

From the start, there may have been doubts that the Trust could achieve what it set out to do, but it was determined to make the attempt. As *Apollo* commented in an editorial in October 1989: 'If Uppark cannot be rebuilt, where should the contents go?' For forty years, before any of the national museums had considered it important, the Trust was keeping works of art together in the setting for which they had been commissioned or collected. In doing so, it had championed the system whereby works of art can be surrendered to the state in lieu of death duties on condition that they remain *in situ* and that a reasonable degree of public access is allowed. At Uppark, of all houses, where the early nineteenth-century arrangement of the furniture and pictures had survived to a remarkable degree, it was essential that the collection should not be broken up or removed from its architectural setting.

Why was it then that some journalists, and especially those in architectural circles, were sceptical while the work was in progress? Their jeremiads tell us something about contemporary British cultural attitudes, and the way in which general architectural practice and run-of-the-mill building trades have become divorced from historical research and specialist restoration. Those who are firmly based in the first camp now have little knowledge of the capabilities of those in the second. The Trust's experience in maintaining and displaying the contents of its numerous country houses, as well as in reviving or pioneering conservation techniques, suggested that the craftsmanship and scholarship were on the whole available to restore Uppark accurately and convincingly.

One of the bonuses of Uppark's repair has been the possibility of demonstrating what is involved in modern architectural restoration and the conservation of works of art. For, although much work of this type has been done over the last decade, many of the finest skills have been encouraged by museums, by the art and antiques trade and by institutions such as the National Trust, rather than by the building industry. It is an irony that, whereas Britain still has some of the most accomplished carvers, gilders, stonemasons and so on, the general standard of building work is much lower now than it was in the nineteenth century.

Many of the craftsmen and conservators involved at Uppark had not previously worked on such a large-scale building contract. The Uppark project engaged talent of high calibre; it also went some way to heal the damaging rift between the building industry and craftsmen, artists and conservators. For the young craftsmen, especially the woodcarvers and plasterers, it was a chance to measure themselves alongside eighteenth-century work of superb quality. For the Trust it was an opportunity to extend its policy of reviving and nurturing the crafts and skills required in the upkeep of its historic properties and collections. For instance, the Cliveden Conservation Workshop, which proved invaluable at Uppark, had been developed in-house for the maintenance of the Trust's own

stone, plaster and statuary. Before the Uppark fire, the workshop had become an independent company with a wide range of outside clients.

Since many of the craftsmen and contractors were new to the Trust, each had to be thoroughly investigated before tender, and once commissioned, fully briefed about what was required. In fact, the necessary extra time was repaid in the excellence of their work and in the broadening of the pool of experts. The bankruptcy of Lelliott, the management contractor at Uppark, however, is a reminder that the restoration was begun when the building industry was in recession after the 1980s boom. This resulted in highly competitive pricing when the various packages were tendered. Some firms which had expanded in the early 1980s literally 'bought' the work (that is, they priced it below the actual cost to keep their employees occupied) and others were attracted by the potential for 'high profile' publicity. This reduced the overall cost, but increased the risk of both substandard performance and insolvency. In practice, there were surprisingly few problems of this kind. To give the impression, however, that the Uppark site was always imbued with positive idealism about the value of the work being done would be inaccurate. The advances were achieved in an often contentious and always urgent context. A modern building site is a litigious place and there were severe penalties in the contracts for delay. Deadlines *had* to be met or the 'domino effect' of delays would have brought work to a halt.

It was Lelliott's (later Bovis Lelliott's) responsibility to manage the programme, and this it did with the toughness brought from the realm of

Left: The Cliveden Conservation Workshop. Founded as the National Trust's centre for conservation of marble, stone and plaster, Cliveden is now an independent company, working for a variety of clients. Its expertise was instrumental in the rediscovery of the techniques of hand-modelled lime plaster-work for the restoration of Uppark's ceilings.

Right: The carver, Alan Lamb, demonstrating the kind of work he had provided for Uppark during an open day before the reopening of the house, June 1995.

building factories and high-rise office buildings. That this urgency and exactitude resulted in high standards is evident; that a human face was put upon the demanding requirements of time and quality is greatly to the credit of Bovis Lelliott's site team, and especially to Ray Carter, who deservedly won the coveted 'Clerk of Works of the Year' gold medal in 1995.

Many of those engaged at Uppark rented cottages in the vicinity; others spent the night in their cars and vans, and some commuted daily. During the height of the restoration, the building was the centre of a varied social life, with people meeting up after work in the South Harting pubs and round about; St Blaise's Andrew Townend, for instance, moved into a house in the village and married a South Harting girl. Altogether, there were over 250 craftsmen, and although not all spent the entire time on site, Uppark seemed almost like a village. The place evolved its own distinctive ethos, quite unlike a normal building site. The presence of artists and women, not usually seen in the English construction industry, and the civilising influence of the house itself, seems to have set the tone. According to Ray Carter, the labourers, rather than 'effing and blinding and reading the *Sun*', started playing *boules* during their dinner time. With his bluff construction-industry background, Carter began by thinking the National Trust experts and the 'arty types', with their concern for the minutiae of eighteenth-century nails or lime and goats' hair plaster, all 'mad'. By the end of the project, he professed himself a 'born-again' conservationist. Indeed, the Uppark disaster and the subsequent team effort was an inspiration to all who took part.

Three months after the fire, the site was opened to the public so that visitors could see the work in progress and appreciate some of the practical problems. Over 4,500 people came in four days; in 1990 and 1991 the grounds were reopened weekly from April to October. The following year building works precluded any public opening, but in September 1993, before the repaired rooms were painted and decorated, 10,582 visitors came in four days. Craftsmen and conservators were on hand to explain their work and to demonstrate carving and plastering.

Although the restoration has received much praise, some aspects of the work, particularly the replica staircase, continue to be controversial. The new roof has also come in for criticism. There are those who think that copying the ill-proportioned Victorian windows, rather than reinstating dormers to the original design, was a missed opportunity. Moreover, the insufficient increase in the grading of the slate courses, from the ridge to the eaves, has given the new roof a slightly mechanical look. Some of the ceilings, too, look rather obviously repainted. But these are quibbles.

After the Hampton Court fire in 1986, the Trust had drawn up guidelines for the conduct of 'hot-work' during repair work. At Uppark the safeguards were ignored, and the builders' negligence caused the fire. The Trust has now banned hot-work, including everything from lead burning

Restoring the roof of the North Gallery at Petworth, Sussex, in 1991–2. The lead was 'bossed' or beaten into shape with mallets, a traditional technique that avoids welding. Since the Uppark fire, the Trust has banned any form of 'hot-work' to reduce the risk.

to the use of high-speed drills. The ban covers any practice that could result in ignition caused by a build-up of heat. There are almost always alternatives, such as the old method of 'bossing' leadwork. Despite the well-publicised disaster of Uppark, the Trust is still the only national organisation of its size to have banned hot-work, which results in the destruction of several historic buildings every year.

The Trust's *Fire Precautions Manual* was already stringent before the fire, and its recommendations for the summoning of emergency help ensured a quick response to the alarm. In the light of experience at Uppark, and with the advice of the emergency services, the manual has been revised and now covers every conceivable disaster, from floods to explosions. Its contents have been disseminated within the Trust and to other organisations through lectures, seminars and films, and copies have been sent to museums and country-house organisations in Britain, Europe and the United States. Despite these precautions, there will always be a need for constant vigilance and continual review of procedures.

The Uppark tragedy has also underlined the importance of insurance cover that permits restoration to the same standard of the original building. Because the clear and pragmatic philosophy for the repair of Uppark was consistent with the terms of its insurance, the Trust stood in good stead during its negotiations with the loss adjusters. As was to be expected, the interpretation of 'full reinstatement cover' led to debate. The Trust's investigation of the building – and the harnessing of the skills necessary to repair it – was not at all in tune with the understandable aspirations of the loss adjusters, whose job it was to keep the costs low. In the end, the Trust's successful legal action against Haden Young Ltd (whose roofing subcontractors caused the fire) rendered these differences academic, for the costs of the Trust and its insurance companies (Sun Alliance for the building and Commercial Union for the contents) were met in full by Haden

Young's insurers. The legal case, first heard in the High Court in 1993, when Mr Justice Otton ruled in the Trust's favour, was finally settled out of court on 21 November 1994. Every element of cost was accounted for and recovered as part of the claim. Thus, the Trust was reimbursed for its entire expenditure of approximately £20 million.

The preparations for the court case and the huge costs of the restoration placed considerable burdens on the design team. The Trust's staff had to acquire the *savoir-faire* to steer between Scylla and Charybdis, meeting insurance and legal representatives with a lifetime's experience in their fields on their own ground. Here, the Trust's Uppark Steering Group, chaired by Julian Prideaux, came into its own. Its monthly meetings provided an effective forum for the establishment of policy. In addition, the Uppark panel, made up of independent unpaid experts from the Trust's central committees, was convened every six months or so to consider strategic issues ranging from interior decoration to finance. This interaction of staff and committee members – whether regional, national, executive or advisory – ensured that the Trust's policy on Uppark was set and monitored by the organisation as a whole.

Quite apart from the difficulty and length of negotiations, the scale of the building project and the speed of its execution complicated the finer points of Uppark's restoration. Since the Trust does not have its own in-house architects, there was a long briefing process to ensure that architect and client were at one. The system whereby all orders to craftsmen had to be relayed through the executive architect was essential, but it made direct contact with those doing the work more difficult. This meant that when a site tour was made, there might be numerous people attending. Attention to detail is everything in the restoration of an old building or the conservation of an artefact, and the one-to-one relationship of client and curator on the one hand and craftsman or conservator on the other is essential in looking after historic interiors. Architects are no longer always familiar with design and decoration, and it was the Trust's staff who knew Uppark and had the specialised knowledge and experience.

At the time of the fire, the history of Uppark had not been fully researched. This was especially unfortunate since the privately owned collection of documents in the Muniment Room was destroyed in the blaze, although a partial transcription of Sir Matthew's account book and photocopies of other papers (including Sir Harry's correspondence with Repton) did survive. Fortunately, there were also the Fetherstonhaugh papers lodged in the West Sussex Record Office at Chichester, and publications based on scrutiny of the family archive.

Since the fire, the documentary research has been completed and much of it published. There has also been some small measure of compensation in the consequent discoveries for the otherwise unmitigated disaster. The original eighteenth-century wallpapers in the Red Drawing Room and

Little Parlour might never have come to light, the eighteenth-century plasterwork behind Repton's bookcases in the Saloon might have remained a secret, and archaeological investigation might not have illuminated Uppark's building history. In the process of restoration, every detail has been the subject of close scrutiny; for example, in the course of replastering the ceilings and restoring Garrard's reliefs and busts, much has been learnt about the way they were made, as well as their relationship to comparable work elsewhere.

Had the fire occurred earlier than 1989, the Trust's response might have been somewhat different. The differences of approach between 1980 and 1989 are worth considering. At Nostell Priory, after the fire in April 1980, for instance, it was not the aim to restore the damaged rooms to their immediate pre-fire appearance. Instead, the opportunity was taken to revert to the mid-eighteenth-century heyday of Paine, Adam and Chippendale. There were some modifications; for example, the new ceiling in the incinerated Breakfast Room was based on an original Paine drawing, but the more elaborate (and costly) elements were omitted. Similarly, the crimson paper printed for the badly damaged Crimson Bedchamber was repeated in yellow for the Breakfast Room, even though there was no historical precedent (apart from its colour) for its use in that room, and curtains were made to match. The Nostell restoration was hampered by the impossibility then of reproducing eighteenth-century methods of flocking; instead of using a synthetic flock, an unflocked damask paper was hung. Nor was any attempt made to reproduce the extremely high quality of the original door-furniture, and the modern replacements are a poor substitute.

Uppark was burnt only nine years later, but the literal and consistent approach to its reinstatement was in marked contrast. The determination to sift through the wreckage, to repair what had survived and to replace the losses after researching the original method of manufacture has already been described. Also, the lessons of English Heritage's careful rescue and restoration after the fire at Hampton Court in 1986 had been studied. Undoubtedly, the strengthening of the Trust's conservation service during the 1980s was a significant factor, and the expertise that the Trust was able to marshal in 1989 was considerable. The Trust's *Manual of Housekeeping* had been published in 1984. Covering the care of every category of artefact, it is a distillation of traditional knowledge and modern museum practice. It was edited by two of the progenitors of the Trust's conservation department: Sheila Stainton, the Trust's first Housekeeper, and Hermione Sandwith, the first adviser on picture conservation, who in turn recruited, among others, as conservation advisers Trevor Proudfoot (stone and plaster), Rupert Harris (metalwork) and John Hart (furniture). These conservators were to be instrumental in the salvage and rescue of objects in the immediate aftermath of the Uppark fire.

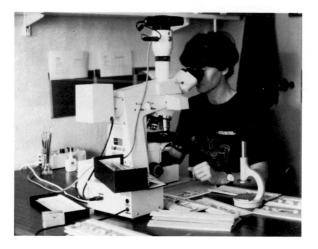

The decoration of all the public rooms at Uppark was fully investigated after the fire. This included paint analysis, the microscopic examination of flakes of paint, which confirmed that the Saloon and Dining Room had not been redecorated since *c.*1815. Here Libby Sheldon, of U.C.L. Paint Analysis, Ltd, examines a tiny sliver of Uppark paint.

In the late 1970s and 1980s, the Trust's curatorship of its properties had developed in parallel to its increasing awareness of its conservation responsibilities, and Historic Buildings Representatives became used to working in partnership with the conservation advisers. Because it was the Historic Buildings Department's knowledge of Uppark's traditions that was crucial in forming the policy for its restoration, it is worth looking back into the origins of the Trust's curatorship of country houses and their collections. Other owners might have taken a different line at Uppark in the face of such a large-scale disaster.

In the early years of the Trust's Country Houses Scheme, set up in 1936 to provide a safety-net for owners of historic houses beleaguered by taxation and rising costs, the Trust regarded itself as an institutional embodiment of the enlightened private owner. There was no concept of curatorial responsibility like that of a museum. However, just as the Trust's Historic Buildings Secretaries (the first being James Lees-Milne) and their regional representatives obtained advice from their colleagues in the national museums, so their roles gradually developed more along museum lines. The importance of undertaking research into the Trust's houses and collections, underlined by the appointment of a professional adviser on paintings in 1956 and championed by the late Gervase Jackson-Stops, the Trust's architectural adviser from 1975 to 1995, also encouraged a more thorough historical discipline.

Over recent years, it has become standard Trust practice to compile an historical report charting the history of each room and its contents. At Erddig, in Clwyd, and Dunham Massey, in Cheshire, acquisition was immediately followed by the study of family archives. Such documentary information was supported by an analysis of each room's decoration, both by 'scrapes', as pioneered by John Fowler, and by microscopic section. This rigorous approach, seen at its apogee at Uppark, derives from a recently

established tradition of country-house restoration in which the National Trust and the Victoria & Albert Museum have both played creative roles.

An early essay in redecoration in the eighteenth-century manner took place at Clandon Park, in Surrey, in 1969. Clandon came to the Trust bereft of most of its original furniture. Mrs Gubbay's bequest of her collection filled the gaps and a grant from Mr and Mrs Kenneth Levy prompted the redecoration of the house. John Fowler's uncovering of original colour schemes and rare eighteenth-century wallpapers, and their careful restoration, was among the first ventures of its kind in Britain. At the same time, Fowler also did some discreet touching-up of paintwork at Uppark, whose former owners he respected for their conservation 'strongly tinged with sentiment'. In this respect, his work anticipated the Trust's present emphasis on the rediscovery and preservation of historic decoration.

The wholesale redecoration or restoration of a house or a room inevitably bears the stamp of the period in which it is done, and this will be the case at Uppark. The Trust's recent schemes at Petworth and Uppark, however, represent both a shift of emphasis towards authenticity based on thorough documentary and comparative research, and an insistence on exact copies of original textiles. They also reflect a desire that the new work should be discreet, and not obviously new: the uncovering of nineteenth-century paint in the North Gallery at Petworth and the matching of missing areas, and the copying of faded rather than original colours of paint, gilding and textiles at Uppark are examples of this approach.

Although Fowler himself had been the first to adopt this line, it came to the fore in the Trust's preservation of the dilapidated North Wales seat of the Yorke family, Erddig, near Wrexham, in the early 1970s. Most relevant to Uppark was the determination that Erddig's unspoilt (and indeed ruinous) character should survive the repair of the structure and contents. Thus, the drawing-room was at first left untouched, complete with cracks

The Saloon at Clandon in Surrey, before and after John Fowler's restoration of 1970. Underneath the late nineteenth-century whitewash (*left*) he discovered and exposed what was then thought to be the original mid-eighteenth-century polychrome ceiling decoration. It may, in fact, be early nineteenth century. After removing the whitewash, he repainted the panelling and remarbled the chimneypiece to accord with the same colourful scheme (*right*).

The central corridor of the North Gallery at Petworth. In the process of restoring the room along early nineteenth-century lines, dark red paint was discovered underneath modern wallpaper. This was restored and copied where missing, so that the gallery now looks older than it did before restoration.

in the wall, and restored textiles were shown alongside unrestored, as they had been by Lady Meade-Fetherstonhaugh at Uppark. The result preserved the spirit of the house to a degree that pleased even its old owner, the eccentric and philanthropic Philip Yorke.

The conservative approach adopted at Erddig was taken a step further in the restoration of Calke Abbey, in Derbyshire, in the mid-1980s. At Calke, not only the bizarre juxtapositions of stuffed fish and fossils with good furniture and family portraits but also the peeling paint in the long-disused servants' quarters were left undisturbed. Most recently, English Heritage has taken a similar line in its restoration of Brodsworth Hall, in Yorkshire.

For English Heritage this marked a considerable change of policy, and the Trust's influence has clearly been felt. The practice of attempting to keep interiors exactly as they were in private hands is contrary to another thread running through recent developments in country-house presentation: this was pioneered by the Victoria & Albert Museum during Peter Thornton's keepership of the old Furniture and Woodwork Department between 1966 and 1984. As well as publishing seminal works on historic decoration, the Victoria & Albert staff experimented with their 'outstations': Ham House, in Surrey, Osterley Park, in Middlesex (both owned by the Trust, but administered until 1990 by the Museum), and Apsley House, in Piccadilly. Basing their treatment of these well-documented houses first on archival research and second on paint analysis, they redecorated and rearranged to emphasise their original appearance and use. In the 1970s the Museum

suggested that this should be the approach at Erddig and Uppark, but much of the romantic 'untouched' atmosphere of these houses would have been lost in the process.

At Apsley, the initial policy in the 1950s had been to ignore the great Duke of Wellington's tiered picture-hangs and to arrange the pictures in a single line more or less according to date and school, as in a museum. In 1980, the original miscellaneous and symmetrical arrangements were put back almost as they had been, possibly the first institutional re-creation in the country of a grand domestic arrangement of paintings. The keeper responsible, Simon Jervis, was later to serve on the Uppark panel, and in 1995 succeeded Martin Drury as the Trust's Historic Buildings Secretary.

This dismantling and eventual reinstatement of more crowded early nineteenth-century picture-hangs, as well as the refusal of the Treasury (on the advice of the National Gallery) to accept pictures of secondary importance, has been closely paralleled at Petworth since the bequest of the house to the Trust (in 1947). At Uppark, the discovery of the picture-hanging diagrams revealed that the hang in the Saloon and the Dining Room has remained unchanged since c.1820. In other rooms, pictures have also been restored to their old places and rehung from copies of Sir Harry Fetherstonhaugh's silk cords that had survived until the 1970s.

In the course of redecoration, however authentic it may be, the synthesis of new work and of contents can sometimes be lacking. Research and analysis are both essential, but they may not be enough. According to

Two houses in the National Trust's care where the conservative approach was adopted in restoration. *Left:* Philip, the last of the Yorkes, in the Drawing Room at Erddig, Clwyd, shortly before his gift of the house in 1973. The magnificently baroque clutter, which included at least two television sets, was maintained up to a point. *Right:* Sir Vauncey Harpur Crewe's bedroom at Calke Abbey in Derbyshire, preserved as it was in family owner-ship. Here the aim was to preserve the spirit of a house whose development was arrested in the early twentieth century.

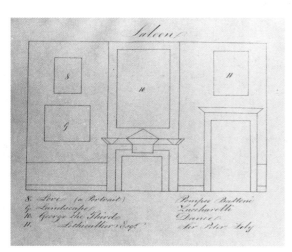

Above: The arrangement of pictures on the east wall of the Saloon, *c.*1820, from a series of drawings that was destroyed in the fire.

Right: The east wall after restoration, showing the reinstatement of the early nineteenth-century picture hang. The brass picture rail to the left was probably installed by Sir Harry, but the pictures were acquired by his father in the mid-eighteenth century.

Gervase Jackson-Stops: '... we should not slavishly follow some scheme just because it is well documented. There may be very good reasons why it would not work today. The contents of the room may be different; the pictures and textiles may have darkened, altering the whole balance; even the original documents (samples of paintwork, wallpapers or damasks) may have gone through a chemical change over the centuries, radically altering their appearance.' Most important is, in Pope's words, 'to consult the genius of the place in all'. Within a room, it is vital to maintain or create a coherent and consistent effect; this was the intention of the original designers, in most cases, at least from the seventeenth century onwards.

To achieve a tonal balance it is essential that objects do not jar with their neighbours or with the faded decoration. A common problem in redecorating is the clash of new gilding with the original; toning down is the normal solution. Whereas museums may tend to think of objects in isolation, in a country house everything has to be considered in relation to its setting. This was the guiding principle in the restoration of Uppark. Given that the restoration's dateline was no earlier than the moment before the fire (with certain pragmatic, mainly utilitarian exceptions), the approach followed lines established at Erddig and Calke, and was consistent with Uppark's tradition. However, although at Uppark the National Trust chose to restore